Love Alone

Love Alone

HANS URS VON BALTHASAR

HERDER AND HERDER

1969
HERDER AND HERDER NEW YORK
232 Madison Avenue, New York, N.Y. 10016

Original edition: *Glaubhaft ist nur Liebe,*
Einsiedeln, Johannes Verlag, 1963.
Translated and edited by Alexander Dru.

Nihil obstat: Andrew J. Moore, Censor
Imprimatur: ✠ Patrick Casey, Vicar General
Westminster, May 18, 1968

Library of Congress Catalog Card Number: 69–16756

Printed in the United States

Contents

Tout ce qui ne va point à la charité est figure. L'unique objet de l'écriture est la charité.

PASCAL

Preface

WHAT is specifically Christian about Christianity? At no moment in the history of the Church has a list of the mysteries which the Christian is required to believe been regarded as an adequate answer to this question. Christian writers have always attempted to find some central insight which justifies the demands of faith, a Logos which if unique was yet convincing, overwhelming in fact, and which breaking out of the sphere of 'contingent historical facts' bestowed on these facts all the force of necessity. Fulfilled prophecies and miracles can all play a part—a much diminished one it would seem since the biblical criticism of the Enlightenment—but they make sense only as pointers within a transcendent framework. This framework was understood in a cosmic or world-historical sense in patristic times, the Middle Ages and the Renaissance, and branches of these traditions are alive today. Modern times—since the Enlightenment—have changed over to an anthropological framework. If the first approach suffers the limitations of a past age, this second is methodologically in error: the framework of God's message to man in Christ cannot be tied to the world in general, nor to man in particular; God's message is theological, or better theo-pragmatic. It is an act of God on man; an act done for and on behalf of man—and only then to man, and in him.[1] It is of this act that we must say: it is credible only as love—and here we mean God's own love, the manifestation of which is the manifestation of the glory of God.

Christian self-understanding (and so theology) is found neither in a wisdom superior to that of the world's religions, based on divine information (*ad maiorum gnosim rerum divinarum*); nor on the definitive fulfilment of man as a personal and social being through the realization of the effects of a revelation and redemption (*ad maiorum hominis perfectionem et progressum generis humani*); but solely in the self-glorification of divine love: *ad maiorem Divini Amoris GLORIAM*. In the Old Testament this glory (*kabod*) appears in the presence of the shining majesty of Yahweh in his covenant, and through this covenant it was mediated to the world. In the New Testament this sublime glory is seen in that love of God in Christ 'to the end' that led to the night of death. A love so boundless (the true eschato-logy), undreamed of by man or the world, can only be perceived and received as the Wholly Other.

This sketch, then, will follow the basic pattern of my larger work *Herrlichkeit*[2]: it will be a theological aesthetic in the dual sense of a study of perception, and a study of the objective self-expression of divine glory; it will try to demonstrate that this theological approach, far from being a dispensable theological by-road, is in fact the one possible approach to the heart of theology—the cosmic

[1] For a discussion of the immanent aspect see 'Gott redet als Mensch' in *Verbum caro*, 1960, 73-79 (Eng. tr. 'God speaks as man' in *Word and Revelation* (Essays in Theology, 1), Herder & Herder, U.S.A. 1964).

[2] Johannes Verlag, Einsiedeln. Vols. I, II, III-I, 1961-5. (French translation: *La Gloire et la Croix*, vol. I, Aubier 1965, vol. II, 1966.)

world-historical approach, and the path of anthropological verification, being secondary aspects, complementary to it.

Consequently 'aesthetics' has for us a purely theological sense: the perception in faith of the self-authenticating glory of God's utterly free gift of love. This aesthetic has therefore nothing in common with the Christian philosophical aesthetic of the Renaissance (Ficino), nor with that of the Enlightenment (Shaftesbury), nor that of Idealism (Schelling, Fries), nor that of the *Vermittlungstheologie*[3] (de Wette). Nor even with the 'aesthetic piety' of Schleiermacher's 'Christian Faith' (para. 9). Some parallel could be drawn with the phenomenological method of Scheler, in as much as it aims at an appreciation of the way reality gives itself to us; but the phenomenologist's methodological refusal to consider the question of real existence (to 'bracket' it) is inconceivable in theology. Our aim is not to achieve a philosophical 'unconcern', based on pure contemplation (*epochê* as *apatheia* aimed at *gnosis*) but a Christian '*indiferentia*' as the only possible frame of mind in which we can appreciate the 'unconcern' and the 'self-concern' of the (absolute) divine love.

We have only considered the central methodological approach in this essay, and have made no attempt to be exhaustive. Such detail can be found in the excellent works of Victor Warnach,[4] C. Spicq[5] and *The Mind and*

[3] The nineteenth-century theological school which attempted to reconcile the profane sciences and Christianity—Translator.

[4] *Agape, die Liebe als Grundmotiv der neutestamentlichen Theologie*, 1951.

[5] *Agape dans le Nouveau Testament*, 3 vols., 1958-9. (Eng. tr.: *Agape in the New Testament*, 3 vols., 1964-66—Translator).

Heart of Love by M. C. D'Arcy, S.J., with their extensive bibliographies.

It should hardly be necessary to add that this essay contains nothing new. It seeks to be faithful to the theological tradition of the great saints: Augustine, Bernard, Anselm, Ignatius, John of the Cross, Francis de Sales, Theresa of Lisieux . . . The great lovers are those who know most about God and must be listened to.

The methodological approach we have adopted is also the central theological *kairos* of our time. If *this* approach does not move our age then there is not much chance that Christianity in a pure form will be discovered at all. This little book may be regarded, then, as a constructive supplement to an earlier essay, *Schleifung der Bastionem*, in which the way was cleared for construction.

Basle, Spring 1963. HANS URS VON BALTHASAR

I

The Cosmological Method

In order to lay the credibility of the Christian message before the world in the most favourable light, the Fathers presented it against the background of the religions of the world. These were sometimes viewed as revealing a great variety (as in Eusebius, Arnobius and Lactantius), and sometimes as presenting a religious and philosophical unity (Justin, Origen and Augustine). Against that background, Christianity appeared as the fulfilment of a fragmented understanding of the universe (*logos spermatikos*) which, in the incarnate word (*logos sarx*), achieved unity, depth and redeemed freedom (Clement of Alexandria). Against that background, Christianity was not only a fulfilment but also a call to conversion, since the fragmented insights (*logoi*) tended to claim absolute validity and sinfully to resist the true Logos (Augustine, *The City of God*). Within this framework of cosmological fulfilment, the relation between the Old and the New Covenants presented a special case[1], since the Old Testament contained prophecies which were fulfilled in the New. Christianity was made credible by being presented as a unification of the fragments, as the redemption of

[1] Although it was not sharply distinguished from other examples because the Bible was read both as the book of the Covenant and as a summary of world history.

the ensnared, and so as the conversion of the perverted. This task was seen to be more difficult if one assumed a static universe (such as that of Dionysius, which left little room for Christ) than if the cosmos were presented as a history either narrated as a dualistic drama (Manichaeism), with a happy ending (Valentinian), or in terms of the Kingdom of God, or the heavenly Jerusalem, fallen into 'a region of dissimilarity' and rescued by the Bridegroom in the course of its pilgrimage through time (Origen, Augustine, Books 11-13 of the *Confessions*), or as Nature coming forth and returning (as in Erigena, Thomas, Ficino, Böhme, Schelling), as matter made fruitful by the Logos, ripening into Wisdom (Soloviev), or again as 'evolving' towards the final nuptial point Omega of Teilhard de Chardin.

This method of presenting the Christian message was made possible because it was obvious to antiquity that philosophy and theology were identical; the natural and supernatural orders were even seen as one thing: God is manifest from the beginning of the world, since Adam, and paganism was a failure to perceive what was clearly recognizable (Rom. 1. 18f.)—an inexcusable failure which was punished by the humiliating idolatry called down upon those who would not subject themselves to 'the manifest eternal power and deity of God'. All the unifying principles of the ancient world—such as the Logos of the stoics, the Neo-Platonic hierarchy of being rising from matter to the supra-essential One, the abstract majesty of the unifying power of Rome—all these were regarded as baptizable anticipations of the God-Logos in person who entered Israelite history, filled the whole world, in whom were the Ideas which were the pattern by which the world was made, and in relation to whom the world could be understood.

The victorious progress of Christianity to Rome, and from Rome to the uttermost ends of the earth, was enough to show that the ideal fulfilment was real too. 'Everything good and everything beautiful belongs to us', St Justin writes (*Apg* II, c. 13). There was, therefore, no reason why Alcuin and the Carolingian school, inspired by the same spirit, should not believe that the philosophy of Greece and Rome was illuminated by the Logos, or why they should not regard Socrates as a disciple of Christ. Why, indeed, should one not find Christian 'consolation in philosophy', like Boethius, since when one contemplated its cosmic glory, one beheld the One Logos? The whole classical world (Plato, Aristotle, Stoic, Plotinus-Proclus) was suffused with the divine, and its picture of the world had always included an image of God. This picture was a sacred one and, formally speaking, lacked only a centre. When that centre appeared and implanted itself, all the cosmic forces of love seemed to have been brought to fulfilment in God's agape, which, according to the Areopagite, could claim the title of the one true eros, and become the focus of all the forces or eros latent in the creation itself. The Sophia of the Bible being made man, became the heir of all things and silenced the desire of all peoples for wisdom (philo-sophial), and so inherited their intelligible unity and rationality. The transition from a philosophical view of the universe to the completeness offered by a Christian and theological universe confers upon reason, strengthened by grace and illumined with the light of faith, a supreme, unifying vision which makes it virtually unnecessary to look for an independent unifying principle for *revelation*.

Written at the end of the Middle Ages, Nicholas of Cusa's *De Pace Fidei* (1453) is only intelligible and justifiable in this framework: for it reaches back across the centuries to the world of Boethius, Dionysius and Alcuin. In the *De Pace* we see Christ, the world Logos, impelled by the intolerable scandal of the number and variety of religions, convoking a heavenly council. Each confession in turn is presented conversing with the Logos and his representative on earth, St Peter, and each in turn is made to see the inner unity of its faith. In all the wisdoms of the world, Christ says, 'You do not find a different faith, but everywhere one and the same faith. For . . . there can only be one wisdom', which is the interweaving (*complicatio*) of all the partial strands of wisdom into their original form. Polytheism presupposes one God; a true belief in creation leads naturally to the doctrine of the Trinity; a true prophetical religion hints at the fulfilment of the Incarnation, etc. Such a consensus of opinion is, however, only possible as long as the background common to all includes a conception of the total otherness of God who is 'always greater' than any idea of him. In the words of Nicholas of Cusa, 'God as the creator is threefold and one; as the infinite (God) he is neither threefold nor one nor anything which can be named. For the names attributed to God originate among his creatures, whereas he himself is ineffable and exalted above everything which can be named and spoken of.' The multiplicity of religions, Nicholas concludes, is in the main due to the simplicity of the uneducated, and is to be attributed to their rites rather than to what is implied in them. The wise, whatever their religion, should find little difficulty in reaching that one Catholic position upon which all their fragmentary wisdoms are focused.[2]

At the Renaissance, the same method was once again to be triumphantly revived: by returning to the golden days of the ancient and fully human wisdom tradition which flourished before their contemporary schoolboy scholasticism and equally incredible monkish abuses, they were conscious of restoring to Christianity its point of reference, and giving it back its catholicity and so its credibility. Dante made the grandiose beginning; then Petrarch discovered, behind the Augustine of the scholastics, the existential figure of the *Confessions* who dreamed of an all-fulfilling religion conceived in a Platonic framework. St Augustine's early work, the *De vera religione*, may be regarded as the model of all Renaissance theology. 'For us who are Christians,' Petrarch writes to Giovanni Colonna, 'philosophy can only be the love of wisdom; but God's wisdom is his Logos, Christ. And so we must love him in order to be true philosophers.'[3] Petrarch and the humanists made monasticism credible once again because they interpreted it and lived it as the truly human form of the contemplative life: from Raymond Lull, the path leads directly to the editor of his *Contemplationes*, Lefèvre d'Etaples, the Huguenot translator of the Bible; the honouring of every pure religious logos of mankind becomes the golden background upon which is inlaid worship of the divine Word (Erasmus's philo-logy); while biblical wisdom and the

[2] *Op. Omnia*, VII (Meiner, 1959), 7, 11, 16, 20, 62.

[3] *Ep. Famil.*, IV, 4. For the historical background see Jean Leclercq, *The Love of Learning and the Desire for God* in Mentor Omega book series 1961; and the same author's 'Etudes sur la vocabulaire monastique du Moyen-âge' in *Studia Anselmiana*, 48, Rome 1961.

wisdom of antiquity are seen more intimately reflected in one another, as in Ficino's *Concordantia Mosis et Platonis*, where Plato is used to give a rational elucidation of the New Testament, while he is treated as dependent upon the Old. As had already happened in the twelfth-century Renaissance, and again in the fifteenth and sixteenth centuries,[4] humanism and the Gospel message mutually influenced one another.[5]

But this return to the pure Logos was, at the same time, as far as the humanists were concerned, a return to the pure word of the Bible, and prepared the way for the Reformation. Then, as the Reform abandoned the philosophical background (against which Christianity had hitherto been presented and seen), the word of God in Scripture and the Christian faith were stripped of their traditional context and framework, and left to confront one another. This confrontation was so naked and radical that the whole question of the *credibility* of the word was dismissed as a side-issue, and regarded as an attempt to provide a human rational justification of the word of God in place of a pure obedience to the pure word of God in pure faith. The great misfortune of the Reformation was that the problem of credibility in its new form was made well nigh impossible of solution in the context of a narrowly conceived and controversial notion of faith, and in a situation dominated by the Western Schism. Nothing could have rendered Christianity more incredible to men on the threshold of modern times than a divided Church: clearly, if the support provided by philosophy

[4] See the works of Renaudet, and "Courants religieux et humanisme, etc.' (Colloque de Strasbourg 1957), P.U.F. 1959.

[5] M. D. Chenu, *La théologie au xiie siècle* (Vrin 1957).

were to be discarded, it was essential to ensure that the unique kind of credibility of the Gospel message should be manifest to others from a living obedience to Christ's chief commandment: to preserve his peace in unity.[6] Instead, interconfessional polemic and mutual acrimony forced the question of the credibility of Christianity as a whole into the background. As a result, the contemporary world, observing these internecine squabbles from outside, was inevitably driven to develop its thought more consistently and radically along the path already mapped out in pre-Reformation times. There is nothing more curious in the history of thought in modern times than the imperceptible shift which took place as the old picture of the world gave way before the new: what was, or perhaps seemed to be, theology only a moment ago, quite suddenly—one cannot tell how—becomes philosophy and rationalism.

The philosophical world-view of the Renaissance was that of antiquity resuscitated—both religious and mythical. By the time of Dante the spirits of the stars and cosmic powers were already being called angels, intelligences or 'gods'—but then as far back as the *Timaeus* the gods

[6] In one of his satirical *Parables*, Lessing describes how the inhabitants of a palace are disturbed in the middle of the night by the cry of 'Fire', and how each one of them wants to save his most precious possession: one of several different plans of the Palace, all of which are said to derive from the original architect. 'Only let us save the plan, each one thought, the Palace can only burn where it is depicted on the plan. And so each individual rushed out into the street with his plan, instead of helping to put out the fire.' They showed one another where it was burning on their plan, but no one bothered to put out the flames, in a part of the building not shown on their plan. 'Anyone who likes can put out the fire at that point—but I'm not bothering' (*Theol. Schriften*, III, 95f.). Soloviev tells a similar acid little story about all Christianity and the East-West Schism (*Russia and the Universal Church*), *Werke*, Wefel II (1954, 184f.).

were seen as 'created' by the demiurge, and fitted into the world's structure. So a cosmos alive with spirits formed for everyone the background to the Christian doctrine of the Incarnation, and it was even possible (in Boethius' *Consolatio,* for instance) to present 'religion in general' on its own without fear that the discerning reader would lose sight of the definitive Christian synthesis.

From this point of view Thomas More's *Utopia* (1516) is spiritually akin to Nicholas of Cusa's Heavenly Council, and so still distant from that 'natural religion' which would contrast its tolerance with the confessional differences. The Utopian's religion is a reduction of Christianity to its simplest, most luminous truths—less some distortions introduced in the Church's history, and with a benign relativization of certain 'positive' precepts. Christianity made 'an unbelievably powerful impression upon the citizens of Utopia when they heard it preached' because it seemed to them to 'correspond most nearly to the faith most of them followed'. There was, for instance, their belief in a religion which made no appeal to force, least of all when it came to disseminating it—a belief which corresponded perfectly with the attitude of Christ; there was the fact that they shared their goods in common, which corresponded with 'the life led in common by the apostles, and so highly praised by Christ'. In Christianity, too, they found the same attitude to God: a pure reverence, a joyous love, zealous personal and communal prayer. Furthermore, they found the same belief in an after-life, the same understanding of death, the acceptance of miracles and the same service to their fellow men performed without thought of reward 'so that the more they gave themselves, like slaves, to their fellow men, the more they were honoured'. There were other resemblances: the number of celibates and monks, the practice of mutual confession and forgiveness, and the obligation to be reconciled with their brethren and to rid themselves of all passionate feelings before attending the holy sacrifice; and finally the consciousness of always living by the grace of God. These and other characteristics are enough to show that the religion of Utopia was a 'symbol' of Christianity, in the same way that the story of the Grail had at one time been a 'symbol' of the sacramental life of Christians. It is only within the framework of this symbolism that the Utopians could ask whether perhaps God himself desired different forms of belief, so that one form should stimulate another. And if, at the end of the book, they once more declare before God that if there is 'a better religion which is more pleasing to him' they will accept it, they do so with this qualification, 'that God is pleased by the multiplicity of religions'.

This whole approach embodies in a humanistic parable what is still only the crystallization of the essence of the Christian World-Logos view, cleared of obscurities. This was the road the 'third power'[7] took, and they[8] were to point all the more consciously to what was essential, as they became disgusted with the bitter ecclesiastical fights.

Yet even the Platonic conception of the world revived

[7] Friedrich Heer, *Die Dritte Kraft, Der euraopäische Humanismus zwischen den Fronten des konfessionellen Zeitalters* (Fischer 1959).

[8] The adepts of the 'third power', those who adopted the Erasmian line in refusing to side either with the reformers or the scholastics of the Roman Curia (Translator).

at the Renaissance was backward looking; in contrast with the growing natural sciences it was already an anachronism. The removal of the gods from their pedestals was at the same stroke the elevation of man. In place of the world-immanent Logos of the ancient world there slipped in unnoticed 'natural' religion, ethics and philosophy, corresponding to the nature common to all races, peoples and ages; one part of revelation was regarded as belonging to this natural religion (in accordance with Rom. 1. 18ff.), while the other part was regarded as belonging to the 'positive' religions (Christian and others), so that these positive religions were more and more insistently called upon to justify themselves before the judgment-seat of the religion of mankind.

The long prepared break-through occurs with the work of Lord Herbert of Cherbury; the knowledge of God and the service of God are severed completely from their Christian presuppositions; they are justified by a self-sufficient religious science, whose formal postulates apply to all revealed religion, genuine or otherwise. As in More, and most of the English free-thinkers of the succeeding period, this natural notion of God is filled with ideas derived from Christian tradition, and yet these factors are regarded as having been found by reason alone, and as rationally defensible. The fact that the 'theo-cosmology' of early Christianity was among the presuppositions of the Christian tradition (which had therefore to be prepared to defend it), made it peculiarly difficult to determine on what level the credibility of Christianity was now to be considered. A sort of hybrid resulted, under the pretence of being a synthesis of philosophy and theology, which prevailed among the more important thinkers throughout this period—whereas the smaller fry were already hot in pursuit of that radical 'religion of pure reason' in which the criterion was definitively shifted from the cosmos to man.

Where, in all this, does Leibniz stand? His understanding of Christian revelation fits effortlessly into his philosophical understandings of the world. If the will of the creator is determined by his absolute goodness and wisdom, the world he realizes can only be 'the best of all possible worlds'. This not only implies a universe of spiritual and rational monads who know and respond to God and who gradually come to reflect his wisdom and goodness; but it also implies that there is a hierarchy of truth stretching from the purely externally believed truths of revelation (*vérités de fait*), up to the eternal truths of reason, which, *a priori*, cannot be in contradiction with revelation as understood; which form the starting-point from which revelation is expounded, and to which revelation must in the last resort lead. Grace perfects nature; God had willed and made both realms inseparable; the individual's uniqueness and his elective predestination coincide in fact. And since each spiritual monad reflects the Whole in its personal inwardness, all of God's plan for the world can be deciphered in each monad in varying degrees of consciousness and clarity. It was Leibniz, that frank and honest Christian believer, who opened the way to German idealism. The cosmological background no longer provided a verification for the truths of Christianity; it had absorbed the whole of Christianity into itself.

Now it is possible, in pursuing this line of thought, to deny every 'supernatural' and 'positive' religion in the name of natural religion; but it seemed intellectually more profound to suggest that the opposition between natural and supernatural contained in the notion of revelation should be transcended; as also the opposition between rational religion and positive religion. It was Pietism which showed the way at this point: an inner, immediate spiritual experience of the divine is itself human, and yet can rightly claim the name of revelation; everything positive, be it dogma or rite, can be understood in the light of this experience. This means to say that while the positive aspect of religion (as *vérités de fait*) appears at a particular relative moment in the historical sequence of events, it can nevertheless be made intelligible and justified in that sequence as an expression of world-historical necessity. Herder was to do precisely this in his *Ideen zur philosophischen Geschichte der Menschheit* (1784-91), where he paints a fresco of great visionary power of the world Logos manifesting itself in all religions and cultures with Christianity taking the place of honour. In *Nathan der Weise* Lessing puts aside the question as to which of the 'rings' (the positive religions: Judaism, Christianity, Islam) was the genuine one in order to consider only the 'miraculous' practical effects of the ethical-religious elements in every confession; and then, in *The Education of Mankind* (1780), arranges these forms of religion serially under the rubric 'development'. Revelation is then seen to be the means of removing the husk and arriving at the inner religious dimension of mankind: "Revelation does not give man anything which he could not have derived from himself . . . but it does so more quickly and more easily.'[9]

[9] *The Education of Mankind*, para 4.

Both themes, the cosmic symbolization of the spirit of God in religions and cultures, and the historical evolution of mythical and symbolic forms, celebrate their triumph in Romanticism and Idealism: in Schelling's last philosophy, where he goes beyond Hegel, both are found for the last time under a Christian banner. His *Philosophy of Mythology and Revelation* harks back to Eusebius's *Preparatio evangelica,* to Augustine's *De vera religione* and to Nicholas of Cusa's Heavenly Council.

During the same years, the Catholic theologian Sebastian Drey, in Tübingen, was writing his *Apologetics as the scientific demonstration of the divinity of Christianity as it has appeared* (1838-47) in which once again the positive 'appearance' of Christianity is presented as the culmination of 'revelation appearances in general'; for as it is of the essence of man as spirit to receive a revelation from the Absolute (thus all history is grounded in an original revelation), so man as an *organic* being receives revelation in two forms: in mythical and symbolical form, and in the form of an historical 'tradition'. Inspiration (prophecies) and miracles serve to bear witness to the 'fulfilment of revelation in Christ'. Once this romantic Catholic theology had collapsed and the frontier between nature and grace had been sharply drawn by neo-scholasticism (Scheeben), nothing was left of the old method of justifying Christianity; the cosmic, historical background, now regarded as (in the main) 'natural', could no longer provide a justification for the supernatural character of Christianity; nor could an historical dynamism, such as Hegel's or Schelling's, mediate between the order of nature and grace. All that remained were the external pointers to the truths of Christianity, prophecies and miracles, while the inward 'understanding' (*intellectus*) of the connections between the mysteries of revelation was reserved to the Christian faith alone.

II

The Anthropological Method

WHILE the cosmological method of verification was gradually losing its relevance, another method was becoming established alongside it, in which the attempt was made to transfer the locus of verification from a cosmos becoming more and more godless (and so having less and less in common with Christianity) to man as the epitome of the world. Formerly, everything had been reduced to a cosmological argument; from now on the same principle of reduction was to be applied, but in an anthropological sense.

At the Renaissance, the image of man common to antiquity and the patristic period was given a new lease of life: man was the 'frontier', the *methorion*, between the world and God; he is seen as God's partner, and the ensuing dialogue culminates in God becoming man. Man is not only a microcosm; with the growth of the natural sciences, he emerges as the author of those conceptions of the universe which in his reason he transcends. That is how Kant was to present him—bringing the Enlightenment to a close. But well before Kant's day, Christianity was measured by the nature of man. Pascal did so magnificently, in a work that towers above all other attempts of the kind: man, to him, is a monstrous chimera, inscrutable to reason, perpetually torn between his *grandeur* and his *misère*, and who can only bring order into his twisted chaos if he looks, as into a mirror, at the figure of the God-man. In Pascal, we have the beginnings of an existential apologetic, or of what, since Blondel, has been called 'the method of immanence'.

The religious controversies of the sixteenth and seventeenth centuries and the removal of the magical from man's view of the world, resulted in a sharp veering towards a purely human and predominantly ethical conception of religion. Christianity is the more easily explained in terms of this religion since both elements claim to be universal and human, and therefore must have a universal inner form. The religion of humanity which this movement produced was a religion which transcended national boundaries and national limitations, and it was therefore understandably accepted by the liberal Jewish tradition, from Spinoza (the *Tractatus theo-logico-politicus*, 1670), to Mendelssohn and Bergson (*Les deux sources de la morale et de la religion*, 1932). Locke, in the *Reasonableness of Christianity* (1695), inaugurated the 'anthropological proof of the existence of God' : spirit can only have spirit as its source and origin. This was followed by John Tolland's *Christianity not mysterious* (1696) and Tindal's *Christianity as old as creation* (1730). Locke spoke of man's duty to measure the revelation granted him by the yardstick of reason; Tolland of removing the outer husk of primitive Christianity—its pagan mysteries (i.e. the sacramental, dogmatic and speculative mysteries)—in order to free the simple, universal message of Jesus; while Tindal resolutely secularized the Augustinian conception of the *Civitas dei ab Abel*, reducing it to a natural religion which honours God and fosters the best in man, and which no priestly authority has the right to tamper with. In these and similar forms, Christ becomes the teacher of a pure truth, and the model of a pure life—while the Pauline doctrine of 'vicarious suffering', and the doctrine of justification become incomprehensible or contradictory (as appears clearly in Thomas Chubb's *The true Gospel of Jesus asserted*, 1738). The first to attempt the impossible feat of reintroducing the teaching of St Paul and Luther into this new anthropological context was Friedrich Schleiermacher, at the beginning of the nineteenth century.

This whole process of reduction was completed by Kant, in so far as he restricted what could be known in the strict sense of the word to a synthesis of sensible perception and concept; anything going beyond this definition, the 'ideas' belonging to 'pure reason', are simply the 'practical' conditions for the possibility of moral action. In acting I know that I cannot act unless I presuppose the categorical validity of a universal ('catholic') norm that altogether transcends me as an empirical subject, and which includes the ideas of freedom, of immortality and of the divine. It is at this point that the unfathomable depths of human nature appear; Kant stands in wonder before them, and the longer he contemplates them, the more incomprehensible they seem to him: 'For there is something in us at which we can never cease to wonder, once we have fixed our attention upon it; this something is at the same time what raises the idea of *humanity* to a dignity which no one could have imagined possible if one only considered *man* as the subject of our experience . . . The fact that we *can* do what we understand quite easily and clearly that we *ought* to do, this fact of the superiority of the *supra-sensual* man in us over the *sensual*, a superiority which will stand *no* opposition in the case of a conflict, even though the sensual is *all* that a man experiences; this moral disposition, which is inseparable from humanity, is an object of the greatest wonder, and the longer one contemplates this true (and not imagined) ideal, the greater it grows, so that those who mistake this *supra-sensual* in us, misled by its inconceivability (it is after all practical), for something supernatural and regard it as something altogether outside our control and not belonging to us and as the influence of another higher spirit, must be excused; although they greatly err . . .' Here, Kant believed, lay the 'solution to the problem of the new man, and the Bible itself does not seem to have envisaged anything else'. This is 'the biblical doctrine of faith as it can be developed by reason out of ourselves'[1], which is called by Kant, 'the pure religious faith'.

All roads of modern thought intersect at this point. In the first place, it marks the way from Luther to Karl Barth —in this sense, that Luther discarded reason (in its Aristotelian form) to make room for faith; but in the meantime this same reason had assumed a Cartesian form and had become scientific reason, the reason which constructs the world. Kant's critique had set limits to this promethean reason, reducing it to a function under man's control and therefore unrelated to religion—which explains why the young Barth called it an 'idol factory' and to that extent the exact contrary of a genuine faith. So too, when Kant went on to regard ethics as developing in the

[1] *Streit der Fakultäten*, I: *Allgemeine Anmerkung; von Religions sekten* (Prussian ed., vol. VII, 58f.).

sphere of the awe-inspiring tension between empirical man and the idea of humanity, ethics remains ultimately one of man's possibilities, although a practical existential possibility. Now unless the Christian faith is to be equated with or reduced to one of these two functions (either to reason or to ethics, both within man's control), it must lie beyond both theoretical and practical philosophy. There remains, however, one other possibility: that the sphere of activity allotted by Kant to the ethical subject should point towards the presence of infinite, absolute subjectivity—in which case the religious tension would be the tension between finite and infinite subjectivity. The question which this at once prompts is: Who is this absolute subjectivity? Is it the transcendental structure of man? That is what Fichte's answer seemed to suggest, and in that case the accusation of atheism brought against him in Jena in 1799 was not unfounded —and then Feuerbach emerges as the one logical successor to Kant, when he calls the tension between man and humanity 'the divine'.

This was the conclusion which the young Schleiermacher wished to avoid. In order to do so, he therefore tried to establish and gain currency for a third function in man, distinct from the theoretical and the practical reason, and which would be independent of metaphysics and morals (these he delivered over to the judgment of Kant). This third function or capacity in man Schleiermacher first called 'contemplation and feeling', in contrast to 'thought' and 'action'[2]. 'All contemplation,' he

[2] *Reden über die Religion* (1st ed. of R. Otto, p. 32—2nd speech). (Eng. trans. of the 3rd ed. only (J. Oman): *On Religion: Speeches to its Cultured Despisers*, London 1894. N.Y. paperback reprint 1958.)

writes, 'proceeds from the influence of the contemplated upon the contemplator,' but this impulse, this influence, is an experienced, felt totality. What Schleiermacher is after at this point is a fundamental, original and indescribable unity of the two factors 'image' and 'feeling'[3], before they have been differentiated from one another. That is why, in *The Christian Faith*, he replaced his earlier formula ('contemplation and feeling') by a new one: 'absolute dependence', as an expression of this primary experience (*Urerfahrung*) of a created being, of being affected from without, which 'is neither a knowing nor a doing but a modification of feeling or of immediate self-consciousness'.[4]

Historically speaking, at this point Schleiermacher had once again gone back behind St Thomas (and Aristotle) as read by Kant to the Augustinian and ultimately Platonic doctrine of the finite subject's immediate 'illumination' by the infinite perfect Good. He describes the religious subject as pure passivity (παθεῖν τὰ θεῖα)—though the notion is now given a more radical interpretation necessitated by the fact that Luther and Kant had discarded 'metaphysics and ethics'—as in due course Barth was to do. Nevertheless, for Schleiermacher, though he unequivocally defines his experience of absolute dependence as an effect coming from outside upon the pious heart, it still remains for him a human disposition.[5]

This disposition is a proper subject for philosophical

[3] *Ibid.*, pp. 42, 46-50.

[4] *Der Christliche Glaube* (2nd ed. 1830) Introduction, para. 3-4 (Eng. trans. *The Christian Faith*, Edinburgh 1948, p. 5, reprinted in paperback, 2 vols., N.Y. 1963).

[5] *Reden*, I, p. 13.

enquiry. In his *Dialektik*, Schleiermacher shows that the inner finiteness of polarity of all thought is evident from a consideration of the infinite beyond our control (and thus our dependence on that infinite); and while he analyses the historical fact of Christian piety, in order to discover the condition for its possibility, he demonstrates that this condition rests essentially upon an effective impulse from Jesus of Nazareth. In spite of this, however, it is from this impulse that he starts to analyse the redemption of the 'pious soul' and its union with the All (God)—starting from the self-same impulse to analyse its consciousness of being fallen and sinful.

Thus everything is determined by the fact that in his dogmatic theology Schleiermacher subsumes Christology under the heading of the consciousness of being saved, as the condition of its possibility. Only in relation to the pious consciousness are dogmatic propositions in general to be called scientific. The historical fact of being moved by Christ could, if necessary, and if it is not to remain purely historical and empirical (and consequently dogmatically meaningless), be understood in terms of Schelling's category, 'the inner historicity of the spirit'; but this would, at the most, mean that our experience of Christ would simply appear as the culmination (the 'revelation' in Schelling's language) of the progressive manifestation of the absolute spirit (in 'myth'). But Schleiermacher would not take this road, though it provided Sebastian Drey with his solution.

Schleiermacher's scheme of thought came to him ultimately from his pietistic forebears, and his answer was mirrored in every conceivable type of orthodoxy and liberalism throughout the nineteenth century, and down to our own times. It appeared once again, in its most recent form, in the work of Rudolph Bultmann. What Schleiermacher calls 'feeling' Bultmann calls 'existence', what was called 'a consciousness of fallenness and guilt' is now described as 'existence in a state of fallenness in the world,' a prey to anxiety and dread among things beyond his control. What was then called an awareness of being redeemed is now called 'becoming unworldly' (*Entweltlichung*) (is this Platonic-Kantian? or Johannine?). This happening to a person's existence is also placed in some causal relation with the historical kerygma of Jesus of Nazareth's redeeming death: the power belongs exclusively to the message, to the kerygma; what actually happened in history can be left out of account . . . as, in the last analysis, it can in Schleiermacher's dogmatic.[6] One cannot 'see' history, and according to Bultmann's theory there is no objective *image* of Christianity, only the kerygma. All we can do is to hear the word proclaimed to us and grasp it in the faith which already holds us in its grasp. Here again, human existence is the measure, because it is the touchstone of faith. The resurrection—of that human existence—is the decisive miracle, the one miracle, as Lessing says, which makes all the rest superfluous. 'Only a man bent upon convincing someone of something incomprehensible need resort to performing miracles—in order to make one incomprehensible thing plausible with the help of another. No one presenting a teaching, the touchstone for which every-

[6] In *the Christian Faith,* all the principal themes are treated under three headings: as 'affects' upon the pious subject; as statements about the cosmos; as statements about God. The second and third headings are derivative and 'strictly speaking superfluous'—See *Sendschreiben an Lücke,* Ed. by Mulert (1908), 47f.

one carries about with him, is driven to perform miracles.'[7]

Catholic theology too felt called upon to follow suit and adopt the same touchstone. It did so at the turn of the century in the 'Modernist' movement, so-called. The central proposition of the movement was the belief that the test of objective, dogmatic propositions was their meaning and significance for the individual and their efficacy to fulfil and complete him. The religious man must, no doubt, undergo all manner of deaths and mortifications and conversions in the process of perfecting himself; these trials are demanded of him by a greater truth in order that he may assimilate himself to it; certainly his relation to God may be understood as pure need and as absolute dependence; but nevertheless, whatever God in his grace reveals to him is to be measured and appreciated by the way it benefits, enlarges, completes and perfects the religious subject.

The principal objection brought against the modernists was that they held that the formulation of revealed truths should take account of the historical changes in the religious individual; but this was of less importance in fact than the primary contention that the criterion of revelation should be determined anthropologically.

The 'dynamism' of the subject may be interpreted, then, mainly in historical terms or pietistically, in terms of the inner life; but it may also appear in the form of a complete philosophical method which provides an interpretation of man defined as finite spirit. This is the method used in the works of Maurice Blondel and Joseph Maréchal. Their thought was anything but modernist, but

[7] Lessing, *Theol. Schriften*, I, 40.

it does, however, debouch into an anthropological justification of revelation. This is true of Blondel in the sense that the active substratum of his philosophy is an abstraction (*le* vouloir, *l'*action) as it was in German idealism (Hegel's *der* Geist, Schopenhauer's *der* Wille, Schelling's *die* intellektuelle Anschauung), and that for him all human goals, lifted up in a restless dialectical process, reach the frontier of the absolute (God), and so compel man to transcend himself and fulfil himself in an unqualified choice: *l'option religieuse*.[8]

Maréchal's thought is similar: the dynamism of the intellect drives a man on from an affirmation of being, which can never be entirely adequate when it is the affirmation of this particular finite being (*représentation*), in the search of an infinite, divine being which fulfils the intellect's *capacitas entis*.[9]

The modernist and dynamist paths undoubtedly have a great Christian past behind them: God in his revelation stoops down to the level of his creature in grace, and desires to move, touch and fulfil him from within, not from without. Historical revelation in the Son does aim at subjective appropriation, at the revelation to the human spirit of freedom and sonship by the Holy Spirit. The Fathers of the Church repeatedly stressed the useless-

[8] The *Carnets intimes* (Cerf 1961), dating from the period when he was writing *L'Action* (of 1893), show, however, that the philosophical (one might almost say the apologetic drapery) concealed a very pure, Augustinian *cor inquietum* and that his longing for God had always been a loving, humble *fiat* expressing the 'indifference' of his heart.

[9] In Maréchal too there is another concern behind the philosophical dynamism: it is the mystic's veiled intuition of absolute being. Philosophy is, then, simply the forecourt to an intuition or, better still, a movement towards it (Cf. *Mélanges, Maréchal*, I (1950), 23f., and the republished early works included in that volume).

ness of an objective salvation, if it were not subjectively renewed and appropriated, as a dying and rising again with Christ in the Holy Spirit. The Middle Ages (St Bernard, Eckhart, etc.) were never tired of repeating the same teaching, and the writers of the baroque period followed their example.

Wird Christus tausendmal zu Bethlehem geboren
Und nicht in dir, du bleibst doch ewiglich verloren . . .
Das Kreuz zu Golgotha kann dich nicht von dem Bösen,
Wo es nicht auch in dir wird aufgericht', erlösen.[10]

St Paul himself spoke of stamping the impression of Christ upon the Christian, and the spirituals have at times gone to dangerous lengths and beyond in regarding the 'holy' Christian as a 'second Christ' (St Francis, for example). The proof of the existence of God drawn from man's need expressed in the spirit's 'capacity for being' also has a long Christian ancestry which includes the name of Aquinas.[11] On the other hand, no one had ever seriously proposed finding the criterion for the truth of revelation in the heart of the pious individual; nor had there been any attempt to measure the depths of grace by the abyss of human need and sin; the content of dogma had never

[10] Though Christ in Bethlehem a thousand times were born
But not in thee, in all eternity thou art forlorn . . .
The Cross of Golgotha, from evil never can,
Unless thou rais'd it in thy heart, remit the ban.
—Angelus Silesius, *Cherubinischer Wandersmann*, I, 61-62, cf. V, 160; II, 81; V, 325.

[11] In the foundations of his anthropology, Aquinas bases the proof intellectually on the dynamism of the natural desire to contemplate God (CG, III, 25), and ethically on the dynamism of the desire for perfect happiness (STR I II, 99, Arts 2, 3).

been judged by the excellence of its influence upon man: the Spirit does not reveal itself, it reveals the Father in the Son made man, and the Son can never be re-absorbed into the Spirit, not even into the Holy Spirit.

There is one other road leading from the Kantian cross-roads and on it we find figures more significant even than any we have yet considered: those who unhesitatingly took the abstract principles of idealism in a concrete sense. Why is the distance and disparity between empirical man and ideal humanity so great if not because no one man by himself can be humanity, and because in order to concern himself with humanity, the individual man must, at the very least, encounter and confront *another* person?

Ludwig Feuerbach (1804-72) was the first to state this quite clearly. Man only exists, he says, if he co-exists; he only really exists in the encounter between 'I' and 'Thou.' The otherness of the other person is the fundamental fact which must be recognized if we are to aim at harmony and community within the community of human nature —which Feuerbach no doubt identified all too hastily once again with 'the eternal in us'; but his conception of the otherness of the other enabled him to re-discover the traditional doctrine of analogy, as defined by the Fourth Lateran Council: 'however great we may consider the likeness between creator and created, we must consider the unlikeness greater still'.[12] (It is true that he only discovered it to dismiss it immediately as a figment of the imagination.) One must start from the *real* man; he is not only the key to nature; he is the proper study of

[12] *The Essence of Christianity*, Introduction, ch. 2.

philosophy. Philosophy is anthropology—nothing else.[13]

'The new philosophy' therefore 'rests on the truth of love . . . where there is no love there is no truth.'[14] Only in love of the other *as* other, only when man passes beyond the sphere of I into the sphere of Thou, can he find the road from man to humanity. This is the crucial junction in history where Marx branches off (going back to Hegel's dialectic) and also the personalists and the religious socialists (whether Christian or not), Ferdinand Ebner, Martin Buber[15] and Leonhard Ragaz.[16] Man can only remain man, indeed he only comes to himself in 'encounter.' Truth only appears—i.e. the depths of the human being only reveal themselves, freely, spontaneously, gratuitously—when man comes face to face

[13] *Grundsätze der Philosophie der Zukunft*, para 54 (1843), *Werke*, II, p. 317.

[14] *Ibid.*, 34-35, p. 299.

[15] [See *Martin Buber and Christianity*, Harvill, 1961. Tr.]

[16] A weak form of this powerful movement is to be found in the common run of Catholic personalism which appeared at the end of the First World War, at the same time as the *Jugendbewegung*. It was inspired by the Scheler of the middle years and a few of its descendants are still haunting us. It is largely concerned with developing 'the Christian personality' in terms of 'freedom and responsibility', and this is regarded as fostered by the free encounter of men, cultures and religious communities, including the Church. In a Christianity of this kind, the Cross is either part of an 'organic asceticism', or is regarded as a regrettable epilogue to the partnership between God and man which began under such good auspices in the (mutual) alliance of the Old and New Covenants. Something of all this is, paradoxically enough, mirrored in the liturgical movement, where a very right desire for more lay participation in the Mass is surreptitiously transformed into a wallowing personal enjoyment of communal piety—a subtle shift of emphasis that is sometimes reflected in contemporary ecclesiastical architecture. There is, finally, a sort of vulgar theory of the Mystical Body, the antecedents of which are to be found in romantic, cosmological theology: sanctified by the sacraments and the practice of the virtues, the 'member' of the Body of Christ is joined to the Head either spiritually (and aristocratically) or cosmically (and democratically) according as the *ecclesia* is regarded as the eschatological Jerusalem, or the incarnation of God in the universe as a whole (Teilhard de Chardin).

with another man; and the depths then revealed are such that Feuerbach, and later Scheler, equate them with the divine. At this point, anthropology moves away from an abstract, dialectical thought towards concrete dialogue: principles no longer clash and resolve themselves, but 'the other' encounters 'the other' in his otherness—paradigmatically in the sexes—and this collision of foreign bodies, this resistance of one to another—instead of overpowering and dominating one another physically or spiritually—forces both to reach a truth above and beyond their finiteness. Whereas every other form of the anthropological reduction ends with a man who possesses the world and God in his understanding of himself—all the more so as the cosmos is emptied of its religious significance—this final form (personalism) of the reduction leads on towards something like a hint or pointer: If God, who is the absolute other, is to encounter man, then the place of his appearance must be that of the man who is to me 'the other,' my 'neighbour,' who is furthest from me because I can never know or experience him in his uniqueness, while at the same time I may know and experience a lot *about* him, *of* him, and *through* him. If God only came to us as 'spirit'—the spirit who is 'more interior to me than my own spirit'—he would not have appeared in his essential otherness. As 'spirit' he only comes to affirm and illuminate his otherness, to give us more intimate knowledge of his 'word,' which comes from elsewhere, from outside, from 'the other.'

But this is no more than a hint. It is not a deduction from the conditions of the possibility of revelation. Its inadequacy appears the moment we consider that however different the two persons involved may be, they meet as two with the same 'nature'—one cannot exclude nature from the study of personal being on grounds of method. There is, in fact, no such thing as 'personalogy,' though we have psychology and *Geisteswissenschaft;* and the mutual revelation of love is co-extensive with the kind of understanding which a common nature presupposes. That is why this last form of the anthropological method cannot serve as a basis from which to understand revelation. The Christian revelation cannot be reduced to a system based on the principle of dialogue.[17] Even though the individual may adapt language creatively to his own personality—it remains a common medium. Between man and God, however, the only language possible is the word of God, that is if we mean a genuine, personal disclosure, and not some vague knowledge of one another's existence; and this communication is only possible if it so pleases God to make his word understood by man, which means to say, if he interprets himself in speaking to man.[18]

And, finally, there are a few other figures who occupy

[17] The dangers of the method appear in Emil Brunner's *Wahrheit als Begegnung* (1938). Cf. the works of Dietrich von Hildebrand, Gabriel Marcel and August Brunner, and the works of Martin Buber based on 'the principle of dialogue' published in the first volume of *Werke* (1962). Karl Jaspers' *Philosophie* (Vol. II, 1932) offers an example of a purely philosophical application of the principle; for further literature see the article 'Ich-du-verhältnis' in RGG (3rd ed.) III (Theunissen).

[18] This should make it clear why Karl Barth, basing everything upon God's word and its self-interpretation through man, inevitably rejects the '*analogia entis*'. It would, however, be enough for his purpose, as it suffices for the purposes of this book, to deny the possibility of reducing revelation to a previous rational understanding of God's existence, of the 'divine'. If one has never met, spoken to, or been introduced to a certain person, but knows something about him, one can equally say that one 'knows' him or that one does not know him.

a position on the fringe of this modern anthropological reduction whose whole effort was directed towards clarifying the possibility of hearing the word of God, keeping within the subjective realm, and yet not reducing this word to the purely subjective. The first is that stalwart opponent of the Enlightenment, Hamann, so single-minded in his pursuit of his fundamental intention, however much the luxuriance of his style may conceal the fact. Hamann's overriding purpose is always to make room, so that the love of God, in the form of the Servant, the eternally inconceivable love of God may be made visible in the act of humbling itself. And then there is, above all, Søren Kierkegaard. He starts from the dialogue principle (speaking at first only through his pseudonyms, the one answering the other, through the long monologues addressed to Regina Olsen, in which he tries to explain himself to her, and finally speaking only with God), 'gesticulating with his whole subjectivity' so that his whole existence should become a sign and nothing more, that he has reached out beyond himself and above himself, has perceived the absolute sign of God in the absolute paradox of Christ. He too, no doubt, says 'subjectivity is truth'; but this means the personal appropriation of the truth as opposed to orthodox or Hegelian or speculative objectivity. The role of subjectivity in Kierkegaard's thought is the reverse of the role which it plays in Schleiermacher. Schleiermacher regards Christology as a function of 'the pious self-consciousness'; Kierkegaard regards religious consciousness as a function of the absolute paradox by which it is seized in faith, a paradox it cannot conceivably develop out of its own experience. And their opposition is precisely defined in 'The Difference between a Genius and an Apostle.'[18] If man were able to become an apostle in such a way that the whole depths of his subjectivity were transformed into a function of the one who sent him, then it might be possible for him, through his own subjectivity, to make the paradox credible in a genuinely Christian way: the paradox that God is a particular man, *this* particular man lost in history.

Besides Kierkegaard, there are one or two other witnesses who belong roughly in the same grouping: Léon Bloy, always on the defensive against the double danger of the pharisaic objectivity of a tranquillized orthodoxy, and a pharisaic subjective holiness (Huysmans, etc.), and pointing with the same gesture as Kierkegaard to the paradox of the Cross. There is Dostoievski in *The Insulted and Injured*, in *The Idiot* and *The Brothers Karamasov;* and Georges Rouault always trying to make us see in the clown and the fool, the head of Christ, 'head all blood and wounds.'

That is the end of the anthropological reduction and its most genuine and existential dialogue form. But, nevertheless, Kierkegaard's sign language is not the last word. For if God's sign cannot be verified either by reference to the world or by reference to men—then how is it to be done? If one considers the history which we have just run through in outline, it very soon becomes apparent that the question is not as traditional as it may at first seem to the thoughtful Christian reader. There is, in fact, no way of 'backing' or 'underpinning' the text of God's word with another text, and giving it another background in the hope of making it more easy to read and more comprehensible. God's word must interpret itself and

[19] In *The Present Age*, Fontana Library, 1962.

wishes to do so. And if it does so, then one thing is clear from the outset: it will not be found to contain what man has thought out for himself about himself and God, whether *a priori* or *a posteriori*, whether readily or after infinite pains, whether from the first or in the course of a long evolution.

III

The Third Way of Love

THE criterion of genuine Christianity can be neither religious philosophy nor human existence. In philosophy man discovers what he can know of the depths of being, while in existence he brings what he can of these depths to life in himself. Christianity is destroyed if it lets itself be reduced to transcendental presuppositions of a man's self-understanding whether in thought or in life, in knowledge or in action. So it would seem at first that the extrinsic and historical approach of recent apologetics must be the only other way. For at least it is not completely denied room beside philosophy and existence since it only seeks support from these in a secondary and supplementary manner: faith completes and elevates metaphysics and ethics when it is faith expressed in an historical kerygma.

Is there then no way between the Scylla of extrincism and the Charybdis of immanentism? Is there not some approach to Christianity which, avoiding the 'blind faith' of the simple (*haplousteroi*) and the gnostic pretensions of the advanced (*gnostikoi*), can perceive the genuine evidence of the inbreaking light of revelation without subjecting it to the standards and laws of the man who perceives it?

Two approaches present themselves, but they converge into one. The first is the personalist approach we have just described. No I has the possibility or the right to master intellectually the Thou who encounters him in his own freedom, nor can he understand or deduce his attitude prior to their meeting. For love granted to me can only be 'understood'[1] as a miracle; I can never account for it, either empirically or transcendentally—not even from knowledge of our common human 'nature'. A Thou meets me as an Other.

The second approach is that of aesthetics. This forms a third area, apart from that of thought or action, and is independent of these. When one experiences startling beauty (in nature or in art) then phenomena normally veiled are perceived in their uniqueness. What confronts us is overpowering, like a miracle, and only as a miracle can it be understood; it can never be tied down by the person having the experience. The appearance of its inner unfathomable necessity is both binding and freeing, for it is seen clearly to be the appearance of freedom itself (Schiller's *erscheinende Freiheit*). If there *is* a finale to the 'Jupiter' symphony—and I cannot guess this, deduce it or explain it from anything in me—then it can only be as it is; its present form is necessary, every note is irrevocable—unless possibly Mozart would change it.

Such a union of the undiscoverable and the highest plausibility is only to be found in the realm of disinterested beauty. What is plausible in the realm of worldly beauty is doubtless caught up in the network of the subject-object relationship which embraces the whole of

[1] The moment I think that I have *understood* the love of another person for me—for instance, on the basis of laws of human nature or because of something in me—then this love is radically misused and inadequate, and there is no possibility of a response. True love is always incomprehensible, and only so is it gratuitous.

nature; mood, sensitivity and circumstance play their part as links; and so the aesthetic sphere, like the personal encounter, can at the most provide us with a pointer, a signpost suggesting the direction in which to look for the specifically Christian. But to a certain extent it is a valid pointer: just as in love I encounter the other *as* the other in all his freedom, and am confronted by something which I cannot dominate in any sense, so in the aesthetic sphere, it is impossible to attribute the form which presents itself to a fiction of my imagination. In both cases the 'understanding' of that which reveals itself cannot be subsumed under categories of knowledge which imply control. Neither love in the freedom of its gratuitousness, nor beauty, since it is disinterested, are 'products'[2]—least of all of some person's need. To reduce love to the level of a 'need' would be cynicism and egoism; only when the pure gratuity of love has been recognized can one speak of it in terms of fulfilment. To dissolve the magic of beauty into some 'truth' that lies behind or beyond the appearance, is to banish beauty altogether and simply shows that its specific quality has never been felt.

The two approaches converge: even in nature eros is the chosen place of beauty. The object we love—no matter how deeply or superficially—always appears wonderful and glorious to us; and objective glory attracts the beholder only by being some sort of eros—which can be appreciated deeply or only superficially. The two related poles were surpassed in Revelation where the divine Logos descends to manifest and interpret himself as love, as *agape*, and therein as the Glory.

[2] Cf. Rilke's use of '*aufzuleisten*'.

The fact that St John calls Christ the Logos in the prologue to the Gospel indicates that the evangelist attributed to him the role allotted by the Greeks and Philonians to the world reason, the Logos who enables us to understand all things; what follows, however, makes it clear that he had no intention of interpreting Christ either by projecting his life on the plane of Greek philosophy, or *vice-versa;* his intention was to allow the Logos incarnate to manifest and interpret himself. This happens when the Logos proclaims himself love and grace (*Charis*), and as such the Glory (the divinely beautiful: *doxa*), and thus precisely as the truth (*alatheia* John 1. 14.). It is in this way that we attain to an understanding as a result of which we perceive a necessity underlying the facts of history and at the same time it becomes impossible to reduce that intelligibility to something provided by man—or even expected by him.

If the root of this Logos were not love—and because we are concerned with the revelation of God: absolute (unconditioned) and so totally free love—then the Christian Logos would have to fit into a series of logoi from other religious wisdom doctrines (philosophical, gnostic or mystical); these all aim at a union of the fragments by opening up the treasure house of absolute knowledge. But, however undeserved it may seem, initiation of a finite person into absolute knowledge can only come about by bringing the knowledge to birth from man, in the socratic style (as Kierkegaard showed of Hegel). But if the root of this love is divine love then its root is the aesthetic one of 'glory' which secures the total otherness of the appearance of the love of God, and prevents any confusion with any other love, however absolute and personal. The plausibility of this divine love is not illumined by reducing it to and comparing it with what man has always recognized as love. Its plausibility comes only from the form of the revelation itself. This form is so majestic that, without expressly demanding it, its perception exacts from the beholder the attitude of adoration.

The majesty of this absolute love—the central phenomenon of revelation—is the source of every form of authority possessed by the mediators between man and God. The primal authority is possessed neither by the Bible (the written 'Word of God'), nor by the kerygma (the living proclamation of the 'Word of God'), nor in ecclesiastical office (the official representative of the 'Word of God')—all three are 'only' word and not yet flesh; the Old Testament too as 'word' is only moving towards ultimate authority—the primal authority is the Son interpreting the Father through the Holy Spirit as divine love. For it is only at the source of revelation that authority (or majesty) and love coincide. All an authoritative call to submissive faith in revelation can do is to prepare men to see the love of God made manifest, and help them to value that love fittingly.[3]

Divine love may give itself with such overwhelming

[3] It is revealing to find that there is no Greek equivalent to the Latin *auctoritas*—which means 'authentication' in the first place, a guarantee, a helpful influence, a weighty recommendation, advice, exhortation, etc., and only derivatively an authentically expressed view, hence a command, authority. *Aidôs* means respectful awe, and *axiôsis* primarily subjective evaluation, recognition, and only then objective rank. *Timê* means subjective evaluation, assessment, estimation and hence a mark of honour, and finally objective worth.

St Paul understands authority as 'the pulling down of every bastion built to oppose God' as 'bringing into captivity every thought in obedience to Christ (2 Cor. 10. 5) in the double sense of obedience to the obeying Christ.

power that man perceives nothing but the crushing majesty of the Glory, and his response is concentrated into a single answer, utter obedience; but both word and answer derive their meaning from the fact that the eternal Person has given himself a finite person in such a way that the possible answer is included in the very act of that giving, whose heart and essence is love.

When faced with the majesty of absolute love, which in revealing itself comes to meet man, brings him back, invites him in and raises him to an inconceivable intimacy, it begins to dawn on man's finite spirit what is really meant by saying that God is the totally-other, 'incomprehensible, essentially different from the world, in and of himself most blessed and unspeakably exalted above everything else which can be thought of' (Vatic. I, s. 3, c. 1). Without this revelation of love, negative theology becomes so empty of meaning that it is ever in danger of drifting into atheism or agnosticism or into a philosophy (or mysticism) of identity. It is here, nevertheless, where the figure of revelation remains incomprehensible unless it is interpreted in terms of God's love, that the totally-other, the ever-greater, *appears* and seizes hold of us *in* the very act of overwhelming us through the ultimately incomprehensible character of that love. Precisely when the creature sees and feels himself drawn towards the heart of God, he sees clearly the irrevocable and inescapable nature of that primary, universally valid relationship between the relative and absolute, worldly and divine being. And he can only endure this frightening shaking of the foundations of his finite being when he has learnt to decipher the figure of revelation—not formally as a 'word', but really, as absolute love. That is the language of the New Testament: love is not just *one* of the divine attributes, any more than man's answering love is *one* of the Virtues.[4]

It follows from the theological notion of *caritas forma virtutum* (love as the form of virtues) that love is also the form of revelation (*caritas forma revelationis*). Nor can love therefore be regarded as linked to fear in a 'unity of opposites'; fear, in the New Testament, means awe, filial reverence, *timor filialis*, evoked by the correct appreciation that *this* was a revelation of love.

That one can really speak of a third way can be seen from what was opposed by the 'orthodox' to Modernism: an integration ('integralism') of abstract ecclesial opinions, which could not integrate the multiplicity of dogmas into a spiritual and intellectual unity, but could only use brute force in an effort to overpower its opponents.[5] This substitution of force for spirit suggests that a genuine solution on the spiritual and intellectual level was at that time beyond their scope.

[4] Whereas in the Old Testament God's word is still only present essentially in the form of a promise; it therefore remains formally in a state of suspension (in the abstract) between election and rejection—with the result that the answer to the promise (faith) is also held in a *quasi* abstract state in which it is distinct from love. The degree to which this form of the word is dynamically already that of the New Testament must not be overlooked. Here too we begin to see—and it will become clearer as we proceed—that a 'formal scriptural principle', a formal 'scriptural authority' (in the sense of the Reformers), is incompatible with the New Testament; for this would involve abstracting the notion 'Scripture in general' from the Old and New Testaments—an abstraction totally inappropriate to the world of the Bible, which in practice confines the scriptural word within the twofold Old Testament scheme of grace and judgment. 'Scripture in general', as a formal principle and double predestination, one can then see, are two aspects of the same thing.

[5] See Maurice Blondel's admirable (anonymous) publication, *La Semaine Sociale de Bordeaux et le Monophorisme* (Paris, Blond, 1910) and Daniel-Rops, "Une Crise de L'esprit: Le Modernisme" (in *La Table Ronde*, Nov.-Dec. 1962).

The 'third way' is unique in that either the form of Christian revelation is seen as wholly that of the glorification of divine love, or it is not seen in that way at all. In this respect, Rousselot's theory in *Les yeux de la Foi* is entirely correct[6]: either one sees or one does not see; but to see the Glory of love, requires at least a beginning of supernatural love.[7]

This does not, however, rule out: (1) the possibility of being scandalized (the refusal to recognize the dazzling evidence and to answer the call to self-surrender), or (2) the possibility of a groping, rational approach to the decisive vision—when reason sees the lines of the kerygma and the Gospel converging on an 'invisible'—that is a transcendental point of intersection which cannot be certainly assumed to exist.

[6] *Les yeux de la Foi, Recherches de sciences religieuses,* 1910, 241-259, 444-475.

[7] No one has written better on the whole matter than Pascal, in those sections of the *Pensées* where he deals with biblical revelation. Cf. my essay "Les yeux de Pascal" in *Pascal et Port-royal* (Paris, Fayard 1962).

IV

The Failures of Love

IN this love of God which man meets in Christ he experiences not only what true love is but also at the same time, and unanswerably, that he, sinner and egoist that he is, has no true love. He experiences both aspects in one: the creature's limited love, and its guilty frigidity. He certainly has a pre-understanding (*Vorverständnis*) of what love is; if he did not he could not make out the sign Jesus Christ. It would be objectively insoluble and contradictory, because here has appeared the love of God in the form of flesh, that is, in the form of human love. But he cannot proceed beyond this pre-understanding to a recognition of the sign without a radical conversion; conversion not only of heart—and with it the admission that in the light of this love one has never loved—but also of the mind with the realization that one must start from the beginning to re-learn what love really is.

Let us take the limited nature of love first. Without a doubt nature brings the reality of love to us from our subhuman roots; for love is built into the foundations of living beings. Cynical or sceptical theories of a 'will to power' or 'a will to happiness' leave the truth of this evident fact unimpaired. We can see the unpremeditated play of eros; the animal's dedication to its young; the individual's renunciation for the sake of the whole. In man this transitory relationship may extend into the spiritual sphere and acquire a meaning that transcends time: the erotic impulse may open the way to enduring faithfulness; so that the natural relationship between parents and their offspring may be deepened into a genuinely spiritual, family love; the dying consent of the individual to the survival of succeeding generations may give rise to the idea of self-sacrifice for the good of the community, the clan, the people, or the State—and a man's death may, as it were, harvest the whole of his existence, binding it into an act of self-abandonment in which there is an intimation of the love hidden in being itself.

But all this implies a particular movement, a way rather than a completed stage. For there are other strong or stronger forces at work, which limit or paralyse the movement of love: the race for a place in the sun, the crippling effect of man's environment, the frightening extent to which he is restricted by his relations and his own family; there is the struggle for survival, for which nature supplies the strength and the weapons; and there is the law of time: friendships that seemed everlasting cool; people lose touch or drift apart; attitudes and opinions alter; hearts are estranged; physical separation is not without its effect; the love that is to survive must be obstinate and persevering. Vows of love that were eternal are broken when the tide of eros recedes or another love appears, or when the faults and limitations of the person loved become oppressive, especially, perhaps, because human love being finite seems to contradict itself. 'Why love only one woman when there are so many others one could love?' Don Juan's intuition makes him ask a question as valid, no doubt, as Faust's protest against the limits of his finite nature. In the one case the meaning of love vanished in a succession of loves; in the other, Faust lost sight of eternity in the very pursuit of 'the moment' in which he thought he could pin it down.

Even within the family circle, love is limited by nature. If it depended at first without question upon the tie of blood, the very closeness of the bond can become an impediment when the spirit begins to stir: too much mutual insight can dull the expectation of the gifts to come. Parents may deny their children the freedom they need as they come to maturity: their horizons begin to close in around them and they already belong to a past generation. All men's activities—farming and hunting, politics and war, household economy and trade, scholarship and scientific research may be motivated in part by love, but love can never mould them completely or bend them entirely to its will: the other forces of human existence retain their independence and their power; and, as Nietzsche pointed out, when man tries to make human love into an absolute, at the expense of his natural impulses, he contradicts himself biologically and culturally. The ordinary level of human existence, where man meets man, is a sort of middle zone where love and self-interest, love and the absence of love, temper one another.[1]

[1] The English Christian freethinkers saw this soberly in the light of their opposition to an abstract humanism founded on love and virtue. Hobbes most radically of all; Locke and the ethical liberals in more temperate terms; Mandeville without disguise. Any attempt to perfect man as a moral being must be questionable in view of man's animal roots, and even regarded as an historical or cultural process it surely implies a concealed (spiritualistic) attack on nature as a whole and its balance. The Augustinian and Pascalian analysis of existence as concupiscence must, in some form or other, be taken into account even on the natural plane.

The death of the individual solemnly reminds the community that it too is in the hands of a fate that encompasses man. The individual may not resist death, he may even accept it as the will of fate, which, in spite of its severity, allows him an inkling of the wisdom and gentleness concealed beneath it—but whatever thinkers influenced by Christianity may have said, it is beyond the capacity of human nature to unite that resignation with a personal, human love. Death may be regarded as leading us into immortality, into a realm where we shall be purified but also judged, and into a realm in some sort divine—but even when the soul awaits a happy destiny the whole process embracing the particular events is not one we should attribute to love. Especially when the image of a personal God fades, the mythical divinity and glory of the cosmos grows dim, and a personal providence becomes more and more questionable. Even under the Old Covenant—where the love of the covenant Lord for his covenant people (with them for all his creation) was the key to the understanding of existence—death and the after-life remained a liminal twilight zone.

Finally, human love is marked by an insoluble contradiction implicit in an existence which is both spiritual and mortal: the personal love men vow one another n moments of exaltation is final, a love that continues beyond death; but 'eternal love' 'for a time' is a contradiction which no one can live. And yet there is no sign in the domestic economy of nature of (fully) human continued existence—if this existence is conceived not in terms of subtle unimaginable soul but bodily. That is the contradiction: for what love means (and yet does not mean) is that the present should be eternal, and yet not eternal (for it cannot be eternal without becoming an unendurable hell). The heart does not understand itself. At the height of its exaltation, love is full of promise, it is open, not closed in upon itself; its fruitfulness is revealed naturally, in the child, though spiritually it remains veiled. Human love, regarded as created love only, is a strange hieroglyph: grammatically speaking, it is an inchoative which cannot translate itself adequately into an indicative. And then there is the question of guilt.

It has already been remarked that it is Christian revelation that really brings guilt into the light of day. It is when we look on Christ crucified that we realize the abysmal egoism of what we call love: when the question is put to us in all seriousness, we say 'no' where Christ in his love said 'yes', and in our lack of love we say 'yes' without a qualm to his bearing our sins: it can only be right for us, if he will do it! That is why God does not ask sinners to consent to the Cross; only that they should lovingly consent to the fearful death of the beloved (John 12. 7; cf. Lk. 1. 38; John 20. 17). In Christ's passion, humanity—whether Christian, Jew or pagan—is stripped naked in the light of its own truth: and the truth exposed to view is such that 'every mouth is made dumb' and 'every man' who speaks of love is convicted 'as a liar'. 'There is not any man just, there is none that understandeth, there is none that seeketh after God . . . they do not know the way of peace; reverence for God is alien to them' (Rom. 3. 4-19 passim).

But there is also a deeper consciousness of failure among men that cannot be shifted into the foreground, where failures are balanced against repentance. If that were so, man could always right his wrongs. But deep within his heart man knows that he is crippled, corrupt and numbed, that he cannot satisfy any code of love, however vaguely defined. He does not dare to believe that there could be such a fulfilment of his being. So lacking in courage is man, that he feels it necessary to accuse some authority higher than his own heart, a heart which could indeed make a greater effort than it does, but is well aware that it can never go the whole way—especially since no one can imagine where that way might lead; no one can plot the stages beforehand; the path is soon shrouded in darkness; and so his sense of guilt collapses into a more natural resignation. There it can rest and be protected from itself—unless it chooses repose in the ethical domesticity of 'guilt and repentance'.

The finite limits of human existence seem to be a permanent justification for the finite limits of love—and since life as a whole cannot be explained in terms of love, love withdraws into little islands of mutual sympathy: of eros, of friendship, of patriotism, even a certain universal love based on the nature common to all men, or on a 'physis' identical in all beings in whose souls there is a common 'logos'. The identical 'nature' that draws two lovers together on 'an island of love' is expanded into a universal principle, and the differences are overlooked. For example, in Buddhism and stoicism, a sort of love for one's enemies does become possible: the other person's hatred and opposition is simply overlooked and only the community of nature and being considered.

The philosophical and mystical world religions all strive to achieve the 'existential' experience of such an identity above and beyond all differences. A primarily rational process of abstraction enables them to overcome the limitations of the finite world and stress the identity of all being. They are essentially 'gnostics', wisdom teaching, thought. They lead towards the absolute which may be called Being (meaning the ultimate element that is identical in all beings), or nothingness (by which they mean the finite quality of all being). These mental constructs, to which inchoate human thought inevitably reverts in search of fulfilment, always water down love and dissolve it in a higher medium; they disembody its incarnate substance and distil from it a peace of heart, a compassion and a benevolence that sees beyond our finite limits—(it certainly seems to be the nearest approach which humanity can make to the absolute)—and they then take this clarified essence, which is beyond the reach of fate, and pour it into particular situations.

It should be noted that this clarification, the result of an abstract process, is a form of knowledge that can be sustained and maintained only so long as one assumes that everyone admits of some kind of univocal being (or nothingness). Such is the case in China and India, in Plotinus and the Sufis, as well as in the abstract world of modern scientific thought. That is why scientists so often feel attracted by these wisdoms. The religious element in these attitudes, whether atheist or theist, is expressed in a certain withdrawal from the concrete, which gives the individual a superior position from which to act—a distance, however, which makes the directness of a concrete love impossible. That is why all these religions and quasi-religious attitudes can be grouped together under the heading *gnosis*: revelation in the strict sense of the word is either superfluous or plays only an intermediate role, hastening or lightening the way to a full understanding of things.

For this reason, if for no other, it is obvious that Christianity—if we acknowledge it to be a genuine revelation—is not primarily, but only secondarily a communication of knowledge, a 'doctrine'. Primarily, it can only be God's action, continuing the drama between God and man begun in the Old Covenant. The content of this action cannot be reached *a priori*, or guessed from any of the aspects of created nature, because it is a free action of the other *as* the other, so that there is no parallel, no identity capable of providing a preparatory bridge for the understanding. The key to the understanding of God's action lies exclusively in the interpretation which God gives of himself before man on the stage of human nature, by virtue of the identity of the divine 'poet' and of the 'actor', who is both God and man, and of the Spirit present in both poet and actor; the Spirit interprets the action to the spectators, drawn into the drama. God's covenant is the struggle of his love *with* sinful man; that does not, however, mean that the struggle can be measured and understood by man. God's love converts, transforms or hardens men's hearts; but that is its effect, not its essence; and it would be a strange lover who wanted to measure how much he was loved in return, by the change, good or bad, wrought in him. What God has done for man is 'understandable' only in so far as it is *not* understandable or justifiable from a human, worldly point of view, and from the standpoint of our fragmentary knowledge: by those standards it is bound to appear 'foolishness' and 'madness'.

It is impossible to construct a speculative system on the

foundation of this 'foolishness'; to do so would be to reinterpret the realm in which personal love acts (the realm of the Holy Spirit) in terms of the Logos, and finally in terms of cosmological or anthropological explanations (in which the absolute is made known to us)—in fact to misinterpret the role of the Trinity in the salvation history of mankind.[2]

The strange situation in which man finds himself might be put in this way: if he is honest, he has to admit that he can only 'think' of God as the totally other, totally beyond worldly being, but in spite of this, if God appears, man's one wish is, none the less, to imagine him as some more perfect or complete fulfilment of the cosmos or of man. This is inevitable, for he cannot cross his own spiritual horizon, which the 'totally other' alone can break open. But if his world really is burst wide open, God's action upon him can only appear as the action of a totally-other wisdom and truth, not only at the moment of the shock—which can after all be outlived—but as essentially thus, and indeed only to be perceived as such under the continuous effect of the 'shock'. The effect will in no way correspond to the cause unless the shock

[2] For that reason it is wholly misleading to interpret St John of the Cross in Hegelian terms, as does Georges Morel, S.J. The unique revelation of the love of God to a particular saint cannot be reduced to general categories (*Le sens de l'existence selon S. Jean de la Croix*, 3 vols., Aubier, 1960-61). It is questionable, to say the least, when Gaston Fessard, S.J., interprets the Spiritual Exercises according to Hegel: *La dialectique des Exercices Spirituels de S. Ignace de Loyola* (Aubier, 1956); for although God's self-revelation in the covenant takes place within the dialectical framework of reason and history, God is after all not the logos of that dialectic—and the thoughtful Christian can always ascertain the fact, even dialectically or existentially. Erich Przywara is therefore absolutely right when (in *Analogia Entis*, 2 vols., 1962) he allows the whole dialectic of thought in philosophy and theology to consume itself—before the mystery of the divine love which it can never fathom.

occurs at the point where experience is concrete—not, that is, on the perimeter of our experience and where one might expect it, on the frontier of death where man seems to pass over into the divine, but right in front of his nose, in the most concrete experience possible: that of his fellow man. A stone which he cannot get round has been put in his way, to scandalize him when he stumbles against it, so that he is made to feel that he is without a foothold.

There is only one way of interpreting the *scandalum*, the pitfall prepared for him by God, unless he takes offence at the offence, and that is to see it as God's love, a love which goes in search of a man in order to lift him out of the pit, free him from his bonds and place him in the freedom of the divine love that is now human as well. Thanks to the dim awareness, the 'pre-understanding' (*Vorverständnis*, Bultmann) which man has of love, he can listen to the message when he hears it and perceive the image to which it refers. Stumbling into the pit, he learns two things: that the love offered him is quite unlike anything he knows as love; and that the scandal exists in order to make him see the uniqueness of this new love—and by its light to reveal and lay bare to him his own love for what it is, lack of love.[3]

[3] The 'cosmological' gnosis of the pre-Christian era was excusable in so far as the word of the love of God had not sounded within their hearing. On the other hand, consciously affirmed, against the love of Christ, as a higher, more comprehensive point of reference it becomes a denial of love to its face, and thus proves itself guilty: John 15. 22.

V

Love must be Perceived

IF God wishes to make his love for the world known, it must be recognizable—in spite of, and because of, its being totally other. The inner reality of love is really only perceived by love. An egoist must have some notion of love if he is to understand the unselfish love of someone who loves him and not regard it as something which, though better than other things, he can make use of. In the same way, a critic must have an innate or acquired flair for the qualities of a great work of art in order to distinguish it from lesser forms or from the merely pretty (*Kitsch*). This preparation of the individual by which he is placed on the level of the thing revealed and attuned to it, is for an individual man that habit of mind (which may be called the trinity of faith, love and hope) which must be present, at least in germ, for a true encounter—and, moreover, can be present, because God's love, which is grace, bears with it and communicates the necessary conditions for being recognized.

After a mother has smiled for some time at her child, it will begin to smile back; she has awakened love in its heart, and in waking the child to love, she awakes also recognition. The sense impressions, at first empty of meaning, gather meaningfully round the 'thou'; the whole apparatus of knowledge and understanding comes into play with its power to perceive and to conceive because the play of love has been started by the child's mother. In the same way, God explains himself before man as love. Love radiates from God and instils the light of love in the heart of man: precisely a light in which he can perceive this—absolute—love. 'For God, who commanded the light to shine out of the darkness, hath shined in our hearts, whose shining is to kindle in us the knowledge of the Glory of God in the face of Jesus Christ' (2 Cor. 4. 6). The very ground of being smiles upon us in the face of Christ, as a father or mother might smile at us. We are his creatures and so a seed of love, God's image, lies dormant within us. But just as no child can awaken to love until it is loved, no human heart can come to the knowledge of God without the free gift of his grace, in the image of his Son.

But before the individual can encounter the love of God at a particular moment in history, he must have experienced another primary, archetypal meeting, which is one of the conditions for the appearance of divine love on earth. This sort of meeting is one in which we understand the *unilateral* gesture of God's love for man, and understanding includes appropriate reception and answer. Were the answer not in some sort adequate, Love would not have been revealed—for it cannot be revealed simply in terms of being—it must at the same time achieve spiritual consciousness. But if the answer were not included in God's unilateral gesture, which presupposes its own action in giving grace, the relationship would be bilateral from the first and we should find ourselves back in the anthropological scheme. The answer cannot be Scripture in isolation; for in contradistinction to the spirit the letter alone killeth; and the spirit of Scripture is God's word, not man's answer. From the human spirit, the only possible answer is the vital answer of love, accomplished in man by the grace of God: it is the answer of the 'bride' filled with his grace, who cries 'come' (Apoc. 22. 17), 'be it done unto me according to thy word (Lk. 1. 38), and who 'bears within her the seed of God' and thus 'does not sin' (1 John 3. 9), but 'treasures up all his words in her heart and ponders them' (Lk. 2. 19, 51). She stands pure before God, his 'handmaid' and his 'lowly servant' (Lk. 1. 38, 48), and she is 'presented to him all glorious and without blemish' by the power of his love (Eph. 5. 26-27; 2 Cor. 11. 2). And thus she is the model of a loving faith that accepts all things (Lk. 1. 45; 11. 28), that looks up to him and is subject to him with reverence and modesty (Eph. 5. 24, 33; Col. 3. 18).

If the love which God poured into 'a darkness where there was no love' had not in the very act of its outpouring prepared the womb for its own coming—for Mary was redeemed in advance by the grace of the Cross, she is the first-fruit of that outpouring of grace—then love could not have entered the darkness.[1] There must indeed be a genuine human permissive *fiat*, corresponding to the divine action: the bride is 'prepared' and 'presented', *parastêsai*, 2 Cor. 11. 2; Eph. 5. 27)[2] by the bridegroom to himself in such a way that the bride is solely 'for' the bridegroom (*Kecharitomenê*, Lk. 1. 28), is offered to him as a sacrifice, is exclusively at his disposal, as we know from the use of the same word *parastêsai* at the presenta-

[1] This is clear if one takes Luther's *simul justus et peccator* seriously.
[2] ThWNT, vol. V, col. 835-40.

tion in the Temple (Lk. 2. 22; Rom. 6. 13f; 12,1; Col. 1. 22, 28).

This (groom/bride) relationship is the basic relationship of love (true because it is true to the facts), and it unites all the conditions necessary in order that man should perceive divine love: (1) The Church, seen as the unblemished Bride, (2) Mary, who is both mother and bride, as that point at the centre of the Church, where the *fiat* of response and reception is most real, (3) The Bible, as spirit (spiritual witness), can only be both the word of God and the answer of faith. A 'critical' study of the word as a human and historical document will necessarily come up against this bridal interpretation of word and faith in the witness of Scripture. The so-called 'hermeneutical circle' demonstrates a formal correctness, even prior to its demonstration of the truth of the content of the word; so that it becomes possible and indeed necessary to show that in the relationship between *this* faith and *this* word, faith is a *fiat* to the content of the word, to the mystery of the outpouring of divine love—the *fiat* of the handmaid of the Lord. But in so far as the word of Scripture belongs to the Church, the Bride of Christ (because she puts into words what has been 'done unto her'), the Church, the archetype of faith, the bride and mother must (4) present the word to the individual as the living preaching of the word, a function (a holy serving office) which, like the Church itself and the word of Scripture, must have been implanted by revelation, into the answer to revelation. This becomes clear as one considers the mutual relation between Church and Scripture.

It is certainly true that God's revelation implants the answer of faith in the creature addressed in love—in such a way that it really is man who answers with his whole nature, with all his natural ability to love. But he can only do so through grace, i.e., because he was granted the power to make an adequately loving response to the love of God. He can only answer under the 'protective mantle' of the *fiat* spoken archetypally for him and all men by the bride and mother, *Maria-ecclesia*.[3]

The full significance and bearing of the act of faith when performed with simplicity and unreflectively, need not have been apparent in Nazareth or to the college of the apostles. The insignificant seed then planted needed the whole dimension of the human spirit in order to germinate. These dimensions are basically present in Scripture, but were only unfolded in the course of time by meditation on the biblical tradition: they became 'a letter written in our hearts' that 'any man may see for what it is and read for himself' (2 Cor. 3. 2-3); 'and my speech and my preaching was not with enticing words of

[3] St Augustine has described the archetypal priority of the perfect affirmation magnificently in the *Confessions* (xii, c. 15; P.L. 32, 833): 'Do you deny this, that there is a certain sublime creation, with so chaste a love cleaving unto the true, and truly eternal God, as that notwithstanding it be not co-eternal to him, yet that upon occasion of no variety and turn of times does it let go its hold, or parteth with him, but rests itself contented in the most true contemplation of him only? . . . For notwithstanding we find no time before it "for wisdom was created before all things" (Sir 1. 4), not that Wisdom, I mean, which is together equal and coeternal unto thee his Father, by which all things were created . . . but that wisdom verily which is created; . . . which by contemplating of the light, is become light: for this, though created, is also called wisdom. But look what difference there is betwixt that righteousness which justifieth, and that righteousness which is made by justification . . . Therefore since a certain created wisdom was created before all things, the rational and intellectual mind of that chaste City of thine, our Mother, which is above, and is free (Gal. 4. 26) . . . O house most lightsome and delightsome . . . let my wayfaring sigh after thee; and to him I speak that made thee, that he would take possession of me also in thee; seeing he hath likewise made me' (Loeb ed., transl. W. Watts 1631; reprinted 1960).

man's wisdom, but in demonstration of the Spirit and of power' (1 Cor. 2. 4). What the Spirit of God explains in our hearts with 'power', and the Church explains dispensing and 'ministering to the spirit' (2 Cor. 3. 8), is simply the love of God poured out in Christ. The Spirit pours forth the 'Spirit of the Lord' through God's Son (2 Cor. 3. 18) for the Lord himself 'is spirit' (2 Cor. 3. 17). And if in the following chapter (2 Cor. 4. 4), Christ is referred to as 'the image of God', the words are not to be taken as a mythical statement because the world of myth has been for ever left behind since the Incarnation. Christ is that 'image', which is not only a natural or symbolic expression, but Word, free self-expression, and for that reason (through the grace of the Word) a Word heard, understood, and accepted. If that were not so, there would be no revelation. There can be no such thing as a 'dialogical image', not even on the higher plane of the word—though it is perfectly true that on this level all the value of the image is preserved, but indistinctly, for it is a level of freedom—something Protestant and existential theology can be accused of failing to see. If the Word made man is originally (and not just subsequently) dialogical word, then it is clear that the level of unilateral teaching and of ethical and religious knowledge has been exceeded—but it is impossible that Christ should have written books 'about' anything (about himself or about God or about his doctrine); and any book 'about' him can only be about the 'trans-action' between him and the man he encounters and in his love redeems. That is to say, that the level on which his Holy Spirit expresses himself (in the Book) must be, if it is to be in any way 'objective', 'in the spirit' (Apoc. 1. 10) where the trans-action of revelation and faith occurs. In other words: one cannot perceive or testify to this love except from within love, and it cannot be observed from the realm of the 'pure logic' of the sciences, so-called. Such a vantage point, that is, can only be within the drama, the action of love itself; and no exegesis aiming to be pertinent and accurate, can afford to disregard this principle.

VI

Love as Revelation

IF revelation were not love, then a purely receptive attitude to things as they happen would be inhuman and unworthy of God; such an attitude is intelligible only if this rejection of all self-knowledge is to further openness to an experience of transcendent love (as faith). Even God's revelation itself could not instil such an attitude in man as an answer to his word. Love can, *a priori* (and thus as faith), only be in agreement with love—not with non-love. But what we have learnt about the Word from considering man's answer in fact presupposes what we have learnt from God's word about that answer: Only because the Word, as love, has already been spoken and understood, can man give a loving answer, an answer which simply means making a 'free passage' for the Word; it is creation's *nihil obstat* to God whose desire is to penetrate into a realm where everything is an obstacle to him and contradicts his love.

The proposition 'only love can be believed' must now be considered (*a*) positively and (*b*) negatively, in the light of the content of the Bible.

(*a*) The life of Jesus was, at first, a life of teaching (the doctrine being clarified in imaginative parables and miracles) and finally, a life of suffering unto death. But the blazing, absolute character of the teaching, that shines in everything he said, promised and demanded, can only be understood if the whole movement of his life is seen to be towards the Cross, so that the words and deeds are validated by the Passion, which explains everything and makes everything possible. If one interprets the Passion as a subsequent catastrophe produced by some accident, every word, not excluding the Sermon on the Mount, becomes unintelligible. It is quite impossible to establish a distinction between a doctrine taught by Jesus before the Passion, with no relation to it, and a teaching put into his mouth after the Passion. The intelligible content (the Logos) of the teaching and of everything he did can only be read in the light of 'his hour', the hour he waited for, the 'baptism' he longed for; in the light of that event in which he fulfilled his prophetic mission and the Old, Jewish Covenant—the mission which culminated in the sacrifice and the supper of the New Covenant.

The whole purpose of Jesus' teaching, whether direct or indirect, is this self-sacrifice, for 'his friends' (John 15. 13), for 'the many' (Matt. 10. 28; Mark 10. 45), for 'all' (John 12. 32; 17. 21), and what is more in the particular form that he gave to it. It is not an isolated human achievement; it presents itself to us as an act of obedience, and as the aim of a life spent in self-effacing service to all men (Luke 22. 27; John 13. 3-17). The Logos and logic of his teaching is drawn from his sacrificial death, and it thus places all his followers—their existence as a whole—under the same sign, the Logos of the Cross (1 Cor. 1. 18), so that, by implication, every Logos and logic would be annulled (since this logic places life under the law of death) unless it is assumed that Jesus' death, which commands his whole life, is, as such, in his final abandonment, the act which reveals 'the power and the wisdom of God' (1 Cor. 1. 24). But the 'power and the wisdom' do not 'withhold themselves' (Phil. 2. 6), they are poured out to the very end in 'weakness' and 'folly' precisely as functions of absolute love, 'stronger than the strength of man' and 'wiser than the wisdom of man' (1 Cor. 1. 25).

Jesus is proclaimed together with his teaching, 'handed over' by it (*traditus*); his aim and object utterly transcends the sphere of ethics and sociology and, in terms of the world, is strictly speaking a nowhere (*U-topos*) into which he throws his whole physical and spiritual existtence unhesitatingly and absolutely. And thus, in handing himself over in perfect freedom (John 10. 18) to death (death as deprivation of God, Matt. 27, 46, death followed by an underworld bereft of hope, Ap. 6. 8; 1. 18), he makes himself into the indispensable sacrificial food for all men (John 6. 51: 'the bread which I will give is my flesh, which I will give for the life of the world'; cf. Heb. 13. 10-12)—and this is not done as an arbitrary act of imaginative genius but in simple obedience (John 10. 18).

The indissoluble union of word, deed and suffering implies throughout a delegating authority, whose existence remains questionable only to those who wish to slander the one employed, 'sent', as a fanatic or, not to mince matters, a madman—an accusation plainly contradicted by the sober tone, the matter-of-fact attitude, and the absence of any sign of fanaticism or of exaltation. Jesus does not talk about his self-surrender in ecstatic tones but in almost colourless phrases that indicate his obedience. Without refusing responsibility, he attributes the whole initiative and the ultimate responsibility and glory to his Father. Having obediently identified himself with his mission, he becomes the personification of it, and in his self-effacement as 'the servant of God' his love for the world is manifested; and, moreover, his majesty and kingship are never more fully revealed than in his ultimate humiliation: 'Yes, I am a king' (John 18. 37).

The kingship of God, who reveals himself as love, is shown to us in the humble obedience of the Son to the Father, and so we are shown that this obedience is essentially love. It is certainly the model for human love before the majesty of God, but more than that, it is the supreme image of divine love itself appearing. For it is precisely in the Kenosis of Christ (and nowhere else) that the *inner* majesty of God's love appears, of God who 'is love' (1 John 4. 8) and therefore a trinity.[7] The Trinity, though to our reason an unapproachable light, is the one hypothesis which clarifies the phenomenon of Christ as he is present in Scripture, the Church and history, be-

[1] 'For he decided, together with the Father and the Holy Spirit, to show the world the Glory of his omnipotence *through his death and not otherwise*', Anselm, *Cur Deus homo*, 1, 9 (Schmitt, II, 62, 23-25). This explains in what sense the revelation of God's love in Christ is 'indirect'. God not *only* appears in man (as the totally other) but in that aspect of man which is most dissimilar to the divine. This sign of contradiction, though veiled for man, is not so for God: it is only concealed from man's natural and sinful reason. If God in his freedom chose to express himself in this visible sign, then for him it is perfectly adequate (and not a 'paradox'); and this is at once evident if man looks at it with the eyes of faith, from God's point of view. Man can then be certain (*certitudo fidei*) that God's love, though incomprehensible to us, has found its most expressive word.

cause it is phenomenologically adequate, and does not do violence to the facts.[2]

If the absolute were not love (and the doctrine of the Trinity is the only doctrine to assert this), then it would be a logos (νόησις νοησεως, absolute knowledge) that either stops short *before* love (adventist), or in modern (and titanic) fashion over-runs it and 'digests' it—which can only be done by falling back into the sphere of 'understanding'—and implies an *attentat* against the (Holy) Spirit.

The synoptics make it quite clear that Jesus, in revealing the love of God, from the beginning trained men in the spirit of divine love, emphasizing that their faith should go beyond their own criteria and convictions. In the course of this outpouring of spirit, Jesus withdrew his physical presence on earth ('It is expedient for you that I go away', John 16. 7) in order that his Spirit and that of the Father might come and, as the fullness of love, fulfil Jesus' self-effacing withdrawal and testify to the Kenosis of Christ. That is why the 'separation by death' (and this occurs on Holy Saturday) is completely surpassed by the Ascension. Jesus will not be 'missed' by the second generation, for 'the love of God is shed abroad in our hearts by the Holy Spirit which is given to us' (Rom. 5. 5); and therefore St Paul no longer wants to know Jesus 'in the

[2] Wherever Scripture intends a revelation of God (as he is in himself) through the revelation of Christ and his Church (and that is, practically speaking, everywhere) then this revelation is necessarily given in the midst of the economic salvific action and not apart from it. To behave as though St Paul was 'only' concerned with an 'economic' Trinity betrays as much theological indigence as that false dogmatic theology which, instead of retaining the form and content of the 'event' of the saving Trinity, elaborates a network of categories in order to explore the inner life of the Trinity apart from this event.

flesh' (2 Cor. 5. 16). However, that does not mean that the time and place from which the Spirit was sent forth is left behind us; it means that the moment and place where eternal love appeared in temporal form has been taken up into a spiritual relationship lasting throughout time: the living, risen Christ (Matt. 18. 20) is present to us in the continual recollection ('Do this in remembrance of me,' 1 Cor. 11. 25) of the self-sacrifice of God's love ('*unde et memores*'), present however, 'until he returns' (1 Cor. 11. 26), which means in a hopeful, forward-looking sense, not merely in recollecting the past. It is only want of faith and want of love that can imprison Christians in their past; the Spirit has set them free for all time, drawing them into the future so that in every act they are forming and transforming the world, moving towards that unimaginable 'image'[3] which is present before them, not subjectively but objectively in all that they do. It is on this 'image' of the 'returning Christ' that the historical life of the Church and of the world depends. The Spirit of God helps them in their search for the integral answer to God's word of love in Christ, which they have to gather together out of the fullness of the creation, and it assists them in their greatest effort (Rom. 8. 19-27) to give birth to the answer: divine love below thirsts for the divine love above and does so until the miracle of love achieves their perfect union (Apoc. 21. 9f.).

(*b*) But there is a very serious objection to classifying 'revealed truth' under the rubric: love of God. Under the Old Covenant, is not judgment the ever present

[3] This 'image', being limitless (it is *u-topos*), can of course have no place in historical thought, which is confined to the limits of time.

counterpart to love? A 'judgment without mercy' (James 2. 13) falls not only on those outside the narrow frontiers of God's heritage, Israel, but more especially on those within; who withstand the burning love of God—a jealous love that elects whom it will. Is not Israel torn in two, cast between Garazim, the mountain of promise, and Ebal, the mountain of damnation (Deut. 27-28)? And is it not said that only a 'remnant' will be saved, and the rest implore in vain? (Jer. 7. 16; 11. 14; 14, 11)?

Jesus proclaims his message of love against the background of that first Jerusalem, irremediably committed to the eternal fire of God's anger (Jer. 7. 20); but in doing so he opens a prospect more terrible than anything conceivable in the Old Testament. For in the Old Testament, blessings and joys, curses and perdition could only have a temporal meaning; heaven had not yet been opened (Heb. 11. 40) and so hell could not exist either—only a provisional Hades, a Sheol. But now that heaven opens, eternal hell too gapes open for the first time. The words are there, and cannot be ignored or glossed over. And the spirit of consolation will make the world realize that there is such a thing as sin and justice, and judgment (John 16. 8). Everything associated with the powers of evil, with seduction, and with Babylon's offence against love will be thrown, with Babel and the beasts of the abyss, 'into a lake of sulphur and fire, there to be tormented day and night for ever.' 'This lake of fire is the second death and into it were flung all those whose names were not be found in the roll of the living' (Apoc. 20. 9-10; 14-15; 21, 8).

The whole extent of man's freedom to oppose the will

of God is revealed when God in the loving freedom of his kenosis descends into the world of despair. The ungodliness of the world is made manifest by this descent: to him, through being abandoned by God; and to the world, that can now measure the full extent of its freedom to resist God in the light of the dimensions of God's love. Now for the first time, 'the depths of Satan' can be explored (Apoc. 2. 24), and a reflective atheism becomes possible; up to that moment, in the absence of a true conception of God, it could not really exist. But when God showed himself in his undisguised freedom, he drew man out of the shell he had made for himself—an all-embracing, divine, cosmic Logos, and exposed him naked in the light of God's freedom—a freedom in which to strive towards the absolute. The Old Testament had been a long, arduous training leading man up to this point: where everything rests upon the free consent of both parties to a mutual covenant from which man, but God too, can withdraw. And it is only when this possibility has been pondered and its consequences lived out that we are prepared for the alternative which so greatly surpasses it; the fact that although God can and will reject, he will ultimately save: 'I have loved you with an eternal love' (Jer. 31. 3). That is why after all the final rejections, the whole of Israel will be even more finally saved (Rom. 11. 26).

The language of the Old and New Testaments is prophetic; it is the language of decision, and in both Testaments it has a formal unity, being spoken within the alliance. But because it is always open to man to misuse God's love, the Bible simply presents both possibilities. The speculative theology of the Patristic period and the

Middle Ages read this prophetically ambivalent language in a cosmological context and systematized it accordingly, greatly weakening its force in doing so. A modern, anthropological theology, focused upon human existence, has weakened it no less by presenting it in psychological and pedagogical terms and in dialectical categories partly existential, partly logical. The all-important fact is that the disclosure of the depths of divine anger is inseparable from the disclosure of the depths of divine love, revealed on the Cross and in the descent into hell. The very finality of God's threat is a protection: in the figure of his Son, God the Father surrendered his greatest love to man, and hence his threat is a warning not to misuse the gift, because behind it there is no greater love to which man can appeal (Heb. 6. 4-8; 10. 26-31). Furthermore, the spirit of love cannot teach man the meaning of the Cross, without laying bare the guilt of the world, for the guilt of the world is revealed on the Cross and without it the Cross is meaningless. In Christ forsaken on the Cross we recognize what we have been saved from, the eternal loss of God, from which, but for the help of grace, no efforts of ours could have saved us. But in learning this before the Cross, we never pass beyond it: we see our sins objectified before us, and it becomes all the more impossible to abandon the one who is dying for us to his fate: so loveless a thought reveals the evil of our hearts to us, the love evoked by the Cross keeps fear alive in us, and the terrifying reality of being abandoned by God (which means for all time) makes us fully conscious that hell is no disciplinary threat, no mere 'possibility', but a reality that Christ knew fully in his dereliction, for no one could have experienced it in the same way as the Son eternally and essentially bound to the Father. Thus both scales of our eternal fate lie in the hands of God: he is our grace but also our judgment; he is our judge but also our redeemer.

As Christians we know that sins committed in the very face of love are infinitely more grave than those committed in ignorance; that is why there is no way of measuring our attempts to love God; we cannot determine systematically how we or our fellow men or the world will be judged. In the place of systematic elucidations which purport to *know* that in the cosmological context a number of people are condemned to hell, and a number called to heaven, or to *know* from an anthropological system that hell can only be a pedagogical threat, and that 'everything' will turn out for the best—the Christian is entrusted with something of incomparably greater value: Christian hope.

Christian hope is utterly different from any purely human form of hope, for neither can it be qualified as uncertain, nor is it based on mathematical probabilities. Like faith, it participates in that universal love which makes no conditions ('love believes and hopes for all things', 1 Cor. 13. 7), and so transcends itself ('hopes against hope', Rom. 4. 18). It is a spiritual, not an instinctive act, an insoluble paradox which becomes intelligible when it is understood as a form of love, or at least as the beginnings of divine love. Then we can see that it is the only justifiable, and indeed the only permissible attitude for a Christian trying to live his life by the sign of the Son of Man, which will 'appear in the clouds' (Matt. 24. 30; Apoc. 1. 7), and will be God's final 'word' to the world, when heaven and earth have passed away (Matt. 24. 35).

We are not therefore called upon to bring hell and the love of God into logical and systematic harmony, or to make it credible.[4] Nor are we asked to justify it conceptually as love (or even as the revelation of divine justice in its self-glorification), for this systematic theory could not exist, depending as it must on a 'knowledge' which is at once valid but outside the realm of love and yet refers to it. We are only asked not to let go of love which believes and hopes, and through these activities is held suspended while letting her Christian wings grow. The experience of suspension includes the experience of the abyss below, but only as part of my own flight. In the same way a man can only speak of his own hell, because he could never consider the possible damnation of some other person as more likely than his own.

A love that contemplated the majesty of God's love on the Cross and was not filled with awe would have every reason to mistrust itself; and the same would be true of a love from which all fear of judgment had been banished: it might be possible to invoke 1 John 4. 17-18, 'perfect love casteth out fear', but this could only be through lack of deep meditation on the agony in the garden before the Passion (John 11. 33. 38; 12. 27; 13. 27; Luke 22. 44).

In the Garden of Gethsemane, Jesus consoled the apostles sharing his agony (John 14. 1), and among them

[4] On the gates of Dante's hell was written: *Fecemi la divina potestate, la somma sapienza e il primo amore* (*Inferno*, 3, 5-6): Divine power made me, wisdom supreme, and primal love.

was the traitor Judas. In his agony the Redeemer made no distinction between his own innocence and the guilt of those for whom he suffered. Likewise any man who binds his love to God's love can no longer distinguish between his own guilt and that of the world, for the sake of which he suffers fear and anguish; the one self-evident fact is that he has every reason to be anxious in his own account.

Anyone who does not turn away at the sight of hatred, the depravity and despair in which men live, and who does not seal himself off from reality, will hardly be tempted to adopt an individualistic notion of redemption and look for a private way out of the evil of this world, leaving the rest of mankind to despair. God so loved the world that he gave his Son, in order that it might be saved as a whole; and in the same way those whom God loves only want to save themselves in company with their fellow creatures and will not refuse to take their part in the redemptive suffering, for the sake of the whole. This will be done, as it is only given to Christians to do—in Christian hope, hoping for the salvation of all men—just as the Church is called upon to pray 'for *all* men' (and consequently to regard her prayer as both meaningful and effective. 'I exhort, therefore, that, first of all, supplication, prayers, intercessions and giving of thanks be made for all men. . . . For this is good and acceptable in the sight of God our Saviour; who will have all men saved, and to come unto the knowledge of truth. For there is one God and one mediator between God and men, the man Christ Jesus; who gave himself a ransom for *all* to be testified in due time' (1 Tim. 2. 1-6), who, lifted up on the cross, 'will draw *all* men to himself' (John 12. 32) because he is 'sovereign over *all* mankind' (John 17. 2), in order to be 'a saviour to *all* men' (1 Tim. 4. 10), and 'in order to remove the sins of *all* men (Heb. 9. 28). 'For the grace of God that bringeth salvation hath appeared to *all* men' (Titus 2. 11), which is why the Church 'looks to the advantage of *all* men, that they may be saved' (1 Cor. 10. 33). That is why St Paul (in Rom. 5. 15-21) can declare that the balance between sin and grace, fear and hope, damnation and salvation, between Adam and Christ is obliterated for ever in favour of grace and in such a way that the inconceivable excess of guilt revealed in the redemption is wiped out by the excess of grace given in the redemption. Not only are all men doomed to both forms of death in Adam, while in Christ all men are freed from death: but still more, the sins of *all* men, culminating in the crucifixion of the innocent Christ, earned a perfect absolution. 'For God hath included them *all* in unbelief, that he might have mercy upon *all*' (Rom. 11. 32).

VII

Love as Justification and Faith

THE sign of Christ can only be deciphered if his human love and surrender 'even unto death' is read as the manifestation of absolute love. It is because his human love is a manifestation that we are prohibited from changing his humanity, making him a hero, a superman or a demigod (as did the gnostics and Arianism, and in our own day a well-intentioned but unenlightened christology), and thus obscuring love as it truly appeared. The arresting thing in Christ is not that he is more powerful than other men (in terms of knowledge and will and other psychic or para-psychic powers that might explain his miracles); but that he is 'meek and humble of heart' (Matt. 11. 29) and desired to be so 'dispossessed in spirit' (Matt. 5. 3) that absolute love might shine through his human love and be made fully present in him. Ultimately that loving attitude can only be determined (i.e., conceived and achieved) by absolute love. When Christ thus makes room for God, he is not revealing his sovereignty, but his obedience to God, fulfilling the commission of the 'Father who is greater than I'. His task, in love, is to allow the sins of the world to enter into him who is 'dispossessed' out of love of God—to become 'the lamb of God who bears the guilt of the world' (John 1. 29)—and my sins.

This is the dogma—the dogma of vicarious suffering, of 'bearing the guilt of others'—which in the last analysis determines whether a theology is anthropological or christocentric. But for this dogma, everything can be explained on the level of a knowledge discovered by man—no matter how much historical tradition may be incorporated in it. The real 'scandal' which it causes is due to the fact that it cannot be dissolved by gnostic explanations; and the fact that it scandalizes us is a sign and warning that we are at the beginning of an authentic faith. For it is precisely with this act that real, unaccountable, inconceivable love begins and ends; a love, moreover, which *qua* love is self-evidently divine. Ultimately, *only* in that act, can one believe absolutely; it alone, *if* performed, is absolute love, love as *the* absolute, an incomprehensible epitome of the totally-other God. 'And we have known and believed the love God hath for us' (1 John 4. 16).

If this is true, then 'the life which I now live in the flesh I live by the faith of the Son of God who loved *me* and gave himself for *me*' (Gal. 2. 20). Faith here means my response to the love that has sacrificed itself for me. An answer which consequently always comes too late, because God's act in Christ, his bearing away of my sins, happened before any answer was possible, before it could even be considered; hence it is the pure gratuity of the act that proves the purity and absoluteness of that love: 'but God commendeth (proves) his love towards us, in that while we were yet sinners, Christ died for us. . . . For when we were yet enemies of God, we were reconciled to God by the death of his Son' (Rom. 5. 8, 10). But how can an enemy be reconciled while he is still an enemy? With God, as we see, this is possible, and St Paul concludes from these inconceivable statements that by our justification through Christ's death, which reconciled us and made us his friends, we will all the more certainly attain to peace with God through Christ's life (*ibid.*, 9-10).

From this it becomes clear that faith is primarily directed upon the incomprehensibility of God's love, which surpasses and forestalls our love. This is the one factual element, the only 'that' (Martin Buber) on which faith in the Christian sense is focused. Love alone can be believed—indeed it can and must be believed only as love. To recognize this absolute and its priority over everything, this is the achievement and 'task' of Faith: To believe that there is love, absolute love, and that there is nothing beyond it. To believe against all the probabilities of experience; ('to believe against faith' as one must 'hope against hope'), against every so called 'reasonable' concept of God, that points to his impassibility or at best to his transparent goodness, but never to the incomprehensible and senseless God of the Christians.

The first thing that must strike a non-Christian about a Christian's faith is that it is all too daring. It is too beautiful to be true: The mystery of being, unveiled as absolute love, coming down to wash the feet and the souls of its creatures; a love that assumes the whole burden of our guilt and hate, that accepts the accusations that shower down; the disbelief that veils God again when he has revealed himself; all the scorn and contempt that nails down his incomprehensible movement of self-abasement—all this absolute love accepts in order to excuse his creature before himself and before the world. It is too much of a good thing; nothing in the world can justify a metaphysic of that order, and not therefore the sign called 'Jesus of Nazareth', isolated, so hard to decipher, so inadequately supported by history. To erect so magnificent a structure on such flimsy foundations is to go beyond the bounds of reason. Would it not be better to be satisfied, like Martin Buber, with the Old Testament, interpreted in humane, ecumenical terms, with its 'open' undogmatic faith? We should no longer need to distinguish between anthropological and theological discourse—we should have a faith identical with Jaspers' 'open reason'. But we should be declaring ourselves satisfied with 'wisdom'—we should have escaped once more by the skin of our teeth, from the absolute, 'scandal' of the Cross.

Man is led into the open realm in which he can love by the love he believes in because he has understood its sign. If the Prodigal Son had not already believed in his father's love, he would never have set out on his homeward journey—even though the love that received him back was beyond his dreams. The decisive thing is that the sinner has heard of a love that could be and actually is open to him: the initiative is not his; God has already seen in him the unloving sinner, the child he loves as his son, and it is in the light of his own love that God considers him and confers his dignity upon him.

No one can resolve this mystery into dry concepts: show how it is that God no longer sees my guilt in me but in his beloved Son who bears it for me; or how it is that God sees that guilt transformed by the sufferings of love and loves me because I am the one the Son loves in his suffering. That is why a purely forensic, legal justification is untenable; it is only valid in so far as it recognizes that God's love makes us into the person we are for him in the light of Christ. Attempts can be made to point out the psychological and theological stages of the endlessly mysterious process by which our representation in Christ becomes, through his grace, Christ's representation in us, and the way in which his love for the Father and for us evokes a response from us—but these attempts reflect only fragments of the process. The deeper God's justifying love penetrates our being as 'sanctification', the more it evokes and strengthens our freedom to love; it is a kind of 'primal procreation' that awakens in us the response of love which may be hesitant and inchoate in us but attains to its full stature through the mediation of the Son's love (and therefore through complete faith in him). For in the Son human and divine love correspond perfectly, and this correspondence, as we have seen, he confers upon the Church in such a way that she can give birth to the Son and his brothers in the world (Apoc. 12. 17). We are incorporated into this 'full measure' (Eph. 4. 13) and to that extent our deficiencies are overcome; we are made able through sanctifying grace to bring to life through Christian action in faith, what we have seen we ought to be in God's loving sight.

The fact that the horizon of the love given to us always greatly exceeds our own, and that the disparity can never be wiped out in this life, justifies everything presented as the 'dogmatic' aspect of faith: It may remain immeasurably beyond our capacity to realize this love which is the truth, yet it is no inexistent 'idea', but the full reality from which (in Christ and the Church, his unspotted bride,) all our striving and strength stems; that is why our act of faith in an ever greater love is necessarily identical with our act of faith in an ever greater truth which we cannot understand gnostically with the help of reason, since it is pure love, a gift which remains for us an inconceivable miracle.

The several 'mysteries' which 'one has to believe' are simply aspects of the love we perceive in Christ: the Father (the personal-other) is the sender who sends in order that the obediential (Kenotik) character of the Son's love may never be lost to sight; the Spirit is the one breathed forth to reveal the freedom and fruitfulness of a love beyond understanding, and to reveal the inwardness, the testifying power, the Glory, and the pure autonomy conferred by that love. It is the essential identity of the three persons in the Godhead which guarantees for it the name of absolute love and—to the joy of those who believe in love—removes it from the clutches of cold reason,[1] 'strengthening those in whose hearts Christ dwells . . . whose roots are deep and firm in the foundations of love . . . that they may know Christ's love which surpasses all knowledge' (Eph. 3. 17-19).

[1] If the Church is to proclaim the message and reflect contemplatively upon it, then God's self-effacing love (*Liebeskenosis*) must be set out in logical terms, but with this proviso: the mystery of love must be the centre round which the conceptual apparatus revolves. The spirit of holiness and love, the spirit of wisdom and of the knowledge of love are one and the same and inseparable: 'Truth and love are conjoined wings . . . for truth cannot fly without love . . . and love cannot hover without truth' (Ephrem, *Hymnen Vom Glauben* 20, ed. Beck 1955, p. 59-60).

VIII

Love as Deed

Love desires no other reward than love in return; and so in return for his love God wants nothing but our love. 'Let us not love in word, nor in tongue but in deed (*ergon*) and in truth' (John 3. 18). To understand this active love primarily, or worse still exclusively, in terms of man's apostolic service to his fellow men would mean interpreting the revelation of absolute love in purely functional terms, as a means or incentive towards some human goal, instead of understanding it as a personal and absolute. To see Christianity anthropologically, simply as an ethic, is to deprive it of its theological dimension. Judaism, which was not (and is not) primarily apostolic, should be a warning to us; the jealous God who gave himself to us when he formed a bond with us, does not, in the first instance, want anything but the faithfulness and love of his bride for himself. We must therefore love absolute love and drill ourselves in it to the exclusion of all the relative objects which compete with it; for unless we are faithful to it, these relative ends become idols. In the Canticle of Canticles, the bride and bridegroom are childless—they are sufficient to themselves, and they are fruitful within the closed garden of their mutual love—*hortus conclusus, fons signatus*.

So long as absolute love is not given this absolute, self-sufficient answer, any form of the Christian 'apostolate' becomes an abuse, a sort of rationalized channelling of love. (This is apparent from the pseudo-charitable objection Judas raised to Mary's 'senseless' *waste*, John 12. 3-8). The true answer is pure 'worship' (John 4. 24; 9. 38; Apoc. 14.7), a pure, glorifying 'thanksgiving' (Matt. 15. 36 par.; Rom. 1. 8, etc.; 1 Thess. 5. 18; Apoc. 4. 9), a form which gives meaning to our whole existence, and to which we ourselves must conform (1 Cor. 10. 31; Col. 3. 17). The highest priority belongs, without exception, to our readiness to serve the divine love, a readiness that has no other end than itself, and that appears senseless to a world caught up in so many urgent and reasonable occupations (Luke 10. 42). The fact that men outside the Christian tradition put the contemplative life before the active life because it enables them to pursue a knowledge and a practice (gnosis and praxis) that sets them free, corresponds within Christianity—though at this point only—to the superiority accorded to a life which is purely and simply an answer to God's self-giving love; in the belief that this love, from which all fruitfulness stems, is powerful enough to draw all needful fruit for man and the world from the disinterested bridal surrender to it.

That is the meaning of Carmel, of every genuine contemplative life in the Church. The word contemplative can, of course, be misunderstood in a gnostic sense (as giving us special or esoteric knowledge) but it really means the life which Jesus praised, the life of Mary at his feet.

Prayer, ecclesiastical and personal, comes before action. It is not primarily a source of psychological strength, an opportunity for 'refuelling' as it were. It is an act in perfect harmony with love, an act of worship and glorification in which the person loved attempts to make a complete and selfless answer, in order to show that he has understood the divine message. The Old and New Testaments, the life of Christ, the theology of St Paul and St John, all testify to this precedence, and it is as ridiculous, as it is pathetic, to see contemporary Christians ignoring the fact and thinking that they only encounter Christ in their neighbour, or worse still imagining that their only task is to work in the (technological) world. They soon cease to be able to draw any distinction between worldly responsibility and the Christian mission. No one who does not know God in contemplation can recognize him in action, not even when he sees God reflected in 'the oppressed and humiliated'. The eucharistic celebration itself is an act of 'recollection', of contemplation and communion in love, and it is the only place from which the Christian can be sent out into the world: *ite missa* (*missio*) *est*. Only then can the 'unceasing prayer' that St Paul prescribes (1 Thess. 5. 17) be performed in action—once again not primarily as a technical exercise as it is in the Eastern 'Jesus prayer', but rather in the way a man is always and everywhere influenced by the image of the woman he loves; or like the Knight of medieval romances who performed all his deeds for the glory of his Lady. A 'good intention' is a very feeble expression for something in itself much more virile, which is expressed in so many Christian sayings: 'In all things may the glory of God be praised' (Eph. 1. 6), so that 'God may be glorified in all things' (Benedict), 'Let everything be done for the greater glory of God' (St Ignatius of Loyola).

As long as our actions are inspired by love and strive towards love, God is glorified. In the same way that life permeates matter and gives it form, living psychic 'matter' pre-formed by the natural virtues receives its final form and meaning from the 'virtue' of love. Both Thomist and Augustinian agree that *'caritas forma virtutum'* is the fundamental principle of Christian ethics. *Caritas* means any encounter with one's fellow man which—considered from the point of view of God's judgment—can be interpreted as a meeting in absolute love, i.e., in the love of God as proclaimed by Christ. Our problem is one of interpretation, of making all the presuppositions and consequences of that encounter visible, in the light of judgment; it is an absolute objective interpretation which we are called upon to give (there must be no 'reading something into it'), and this is plain from the judgment given in Matthew 25: 'Verily, I say unto you, inasmuch as you have (not) done (the work of love) to the least of these by brethren, you have (not) done it to me'. This judgment astounds both those who have, and those who have not acted. (When, Lord, did we see you hungry . . . or thirsty . . . or as a banished alien . . . or naked and sick and in prison) (vv. 37-40, 45). For no one succeeds in directing all his action upon Christ except Christ himself; and if we live in a loving faith, our ethical standard in the end is taken away from us and our judgment taken into the love of God.

When the believer encounters his neighbour, who, in the context of faith, is the object of his action, nothing less is implied than revelation itself, and therefore the whole of *dogmatics*. Dogmatics supplies the conditions for Christian action in the light of revelation—which here can only be very briefly suggested. Where Christian action is concerned, every dogmatic proposition is indispensable even though the acting agent does not know it explicitly, or knowing it does not perceive its relevance to the existential situation. Christian action is above all a secondary answer to the primary action of God upon man: ('I forgave thee all thy debt; shouldest not thou also have had compassion on thy fellow servant?' Matt. 18. 32). If God had not acted first, our deed would have to be measured by purely human standards and we should then have to take into consideration as well the unavoidable limitations imposed by social life, by the conflict of interests (*suum cuique*) and possibly, indeed, the superiority of the one who forgives over the one forgiven, who may be unworthy of such generosity—ethically a very problematical consideration. But if we assume God's immeasurable forgiveness in advance, there are no limits to human kindness, and the dangers of pride are banished: I am in the first place one humbled by God's own love, for 'the whole of my guilt is to be forgiven', and my own acts of forgiveness are only an echo, nothing more than simple obedience, and in no sense a form of superiority and sovereignty. All the boundaries are erased: For since God forgave me when I was still his enemy (Rom. 5. 10), I must forgive my fellow creatures, when they are still my enemies; and since God's gifts to me—extending to the point of losing himself (Matt. 27. 46)—were 'uncalculated', I must now forgo reckoning the balance between giving and a tangible reward (Matt. 6. 1-4; 6. 19-34). God's measure must become my measure, according to which I shall be judged —this is not 'mere justice', but the logic of absolute love; once again, it is the absolute nature of what has been done to us, and what we must do in return, that is 'fearful'.

Moved by God's act, the believer cannot but act in response; with that in mind, his action is therefore essentially eschatological or, since the word is charged with implications, let us say 'parousial'—the believer acts under the rubric of the second coming of Christ, the (timeless) and, from a Christian standpoint necessary, final act of all his acts in time, when he comes in the Glory of his revealed love which judges and rectifies all things. Action is a forward movement, and action inspired by the absolute is orientated towards the absolute future which is both in and beyond history (Paul Schütz).[1] That is why even the 'least' encounter or an encounter with 'the least' of my brothers comes under judgment. Christ bore and forgave this 'least' and in faith and in love I must see him in terms of that image, of what he is in the eyes of the Father; that is the one true image and mine, however evident it may seem, is false. The Christian meets Christ *in* his neighbour, he does not perceive him behind or beyond his neighbour: that is the formulation that entirely fits the incarnate and suffering love of Christ who called himself Son of Man—without the article (John 5. 27)—and is close to us in anyone who comes towards us.

[1] God himself, as Creator and Redeemer, thinks and acts progressively in this sense: in the light of the final image which 'hovers before him' God loves us, not as we are, on account of our own merit, but as we *will be* as a result of his gift (Prosper, in the Second Council of Orange, c. 12, Dz. 185).

The twofold unity that I find in 'any man' and 'Son of Man' can only be resolved in faith by seeing the individual's sin in the Son of Man, where it is given its true place—because 'God made him one with the sinfulness of man, so that in him we might be one with the goodness of God himself' (2 Cor. 5. 21)—and by seeing in man himself the righteousness of Christ, as the truth which is given to that man as the goal of his life. This twofold unity must, therefore be read in the light of the Cross (*übers Kreuz*), but in such a way that the guilt is paid for on the Cross, because it is transformed out of love into love. The eyes with which to see my neighbour in this way are given me only in faith: faith that I too live in God through the power of Christ's death for me, and must therefore interpret all things according to the prescriptions of this love.

Justification through faith, where both 'I' and 'Thou' are concerned, is the condition of any Christian encounter whatsoever, and it therefore implies everything objectively implied by justification: for example, it implies an attitude of blind obedience on the part of the Christian, who, solely because he is able to transcend the evidence of his senses and of his own psychology, sees the image of Christ appearing in the other man; it implies prayer, because every existential conversation with another presupposes that both 'I' and 'Thou' are embraced in the word of God and in the love of the Trinity, in the 'converse' of the incarnate Son with the Father, in which the precipitous difference between the world as it is and as it should be for God is endured to the end, the responsibility accepted for it and, in the final existential gift of God's word, the difference wiped out. It is only by virtue of this divine relationship that we need never be discouraged or tempted to break off relations with our neighbour, when it seems that 'there is nothing more to be done for him'; for it is through this relationship, the profoundest of Christian mysteries, that the disparity between the heavenly and worldly standpoint is balanced—through the 'indifference' of the Son to the will of the Father and the Father's 'deference' to the will of the Son (John 17. 24).

When we abandon our neighbour to God he continues to be supported by our love and the pain of being unable to help him accomplishes more than any self-confident action. That is why Theresa of Lisieux regarded the contemplative Carmelite vocation as the most fruitful of apostolates. Looking at everything in the light of Christ's love does not mean failing to see or denying one's neighbour's faults; the Samaritan had to see the wounds he stopped to heal. ('*Voir sans regarder*', St Francis de Sales says.) A teacher must acquaint himself with a pupil's degree of knowledge and ability in order to be able to do his work; in the same way the Christian must see the opposition to God 'realistically' (in fact only the Christian will be able to measure its full depth—in the light of the Cross) and yet contemplate it only on the Cross where it has already been conquered (John 21. 31; 16. 33).

Christian action means being taken through grace into God's action, and loving with God, the sole condition in which a (Christian) *knowledge of God* is possible, for 'whoever does not love, does not know God, for God is love' (1 John 4. 8). Love here means that unconditional commitment which implicitly includes (if it should be necessary) the willingness to give one's life: 'Greater love has no man than this, that he lay down his life for his friends' (John 15. 13). 'This is how we have come to know love, that he gave up his life for us, and so we also must give up our lives for the brethren' (1 John 3. 16). To join in doing what has already been done in its fullness, and to realize and fulfil what has been realized and fulfilled, is the fundamental law of Christian ethics, and even of Christian knowledge; for it is only then that what is in itself manifest, is made manifest to us: 'Beloved, if God so loved us, we ought also to love one another. No man has ever seen God (but) if we love one another, God abides in us and his love is perfected in us' (τετελειομένη, 1 John 4. 11-12). This explains why St John emphasizes the reciprocal character of love almost to the point of exclusion (John 13. 34-35, 15. 12-13, 17)—in contradistinction to the synoptics, who seem to stress love of one's enemies, a love squandered where there is no response. There is no other way of showing that Christian love always presupposes the love of the Trinity—St John shows the truth of this principle, in an extreme case, when he includes the enemy and his darkness in the eucharistic community of light (John 13. 23-30).

We have already seen how *ecclesiology and mariology* form part of the basic structure of revelation. Here, they reappear as the conditions of Christian action. It is not we, as individuals, who present the standard of absolute love in human form: we cannot claim to monopolize its spirit; we can only participate in it as feeble, failing members of a greater whole: whatever is impure and fallible in us, is pure and infallible in the innermost heart of the Church. Our obedience in faith to the absolute standard is embodied in our relation to the Church (both the bride of Christ and our mother). As members of the Church we take part in her perfect loving obedience, by being obedient to the whole. But because our obedience to her is identical in essence with her obedience to the Lord, far from being an intermediary between us and Christ, she is an essential step in the process of our integration on our way to the Parousia. Her sacraments articulate the love of the bridegroom for the bride; the recipient of this love is always the individual believer; he receives it directly, without mediation, in the company of the community. The role of the servant (deacon) who dispenses and 'ministers' (or in the case of marriage, mutually receives and administers) is to make this love immediate in a social setting; but at the same time, as has been said, he represents the majesty and the normative ('legal') validity of God's love which is authoritative and transcends the individual sphere.

But the Church is not only the norm legally, she is also the norm for the relation between bride and bridegroom. She not only represents it in terms of a canonical standard, on the level of her absolute purity (as required by Eph. 5. 27), she also represents the norm on the level of, and in the lives of those who approach its perfection, and merit in consequence being raised to the level of canons—being 'canonized'. Those who live a life of total love are not only moral examples of Christian action, but having surrendered themselves to the Redeemer's fruitful love, they intercede for us and become our chosen helpers. From their exalted position, they simply point to the total and mutual integration of the deeds of those who love; their existence and achievements are boundlessly open to one another and constitute the 'communion of saints'. From this point of view every Christian encounter occurs within such a community, and both Christ and the Church give a real mandate (*missio*) to represent the whole community and the whole idea of love within a particular situation. This is the categorical imperative in Christian terms, by virtue of which absolute love, as 'duty', transcends individual 'inclination' and is orientated towards the absolute, as implacably as the Cross of Christ, and with the fire of the living Christ. 'His eyes were as a flame of fire; and his feet burnished bronze . . . and his voice as the sound of many waters . . . and out of his mouth went a sharp two-edged sword; and his countenance was as the sun shining with full strength. And when I saw him, I fell at his feet as dead' (Apoc. 1. 14-17). The vision of the beloved disciple already reflects the burning ardour of the Gospel, embracing and surpassing that of the Old Testament. The impatience of God's love is concealed behind the patience and the poverty in which his love appears, and that is why, when it bursts forth, it does so all the more mysteriously (like the thunder on Sinai concealed in the gentle flame on Horeb).

The saints have always felt something of that categorical imperative and their lives and actions testify to the fact. In them, Christian love becomes credible. They are guiding stars for others. The desire of one and all is only to point away from themselves, to love. Thus whenever the gap between absolute love and those pointing towards it is in any way minimized, and some kind of 'identity' implied or established (as when St Francis is presented as an *alter Christus*, or even the priest referred to as '*alter Christus*')—whenever that false equation appears, whether in a pietistic, spiritual or mystical framework, the love revealed in the Bible ceases to be credible. Such pious misconceptions and exaggerations merely turn Christianity into an anthropological phenomenon; the love of the 'saints' would then hang like a beautiful, heavily embroidered mantle round their fully developed 'religious personalities', and would suggest that they are in search of their own perfection, looking to their own honour, and if only surreptitiously, coming in their own name (John 5. 41f.); the 'eternal in man' (to recall Scheler's title) would appear as a sort of golden background—though as Scheler himself showed later, 'the eternal in man' is always on the point of turning turtle and revealing itself as 'the eternal man.'

The real saints wanted only one thing, the greater glory of the love of God: that is the one condition for all their deeds, and to imagine one knows better and to regard their actions as performed for their own glory, is to contradict them flatly. They are hidden in God, have no foothold of their own. They grow in stature, not round their own centre but round God, whose incomprehensible grace gives ever greater personal freedom to the creature who frees himself to exist solely for God: a paradox that can only be solved as one begins to realize that God, in his self-surrender, is love, as jealous as he is un-envying, as exclusively desirous to gather us to himself as he is to distribute himself universally.

According to Christ himself the Church which he founded is only credible in the saints, in those who tried to make the love of Christ the basis of everything. It is they who reveal what the Church 'really' is in its authentic state; while sinners who do not seriously believe in God's love only obscure it: they turn it into an entirely superfluous puzzle which is understandably the occasion of scandal, and tempts men to blasphemy (Rom. 3. 24). Christ's apologetic can be summed up in a few words: 'As I have loved you, so must you love one another. If you love one another then everyone will see that you are my disciples' (John 13. 34-35); and that is the proof of the doctrine: 'I in them, and thou in me, that they may be made perfect in one; and that the world may know that thou hast sent me, and hast loved them as thou hast loved me' (John 17. 23). Love as action, that is the 'proof of spirit and power'—a love which is truly human, with its centre of gravity in 'the corporal works of mercy', and truly divine because, founded by God's patience and humility, it becomes effective through the Church—through sermon, Mass, sacraments, organization and canon law.

It is only after having spoken of love as deed that one can go on to speak—in a sort of rapturous epilogue—of the *magnum mysterium* of 'the one flesh' (Eph. 5. 31), as joined to the Lord 'in one spirit' (1 Cor. 6. 17), 'One bread and one Body' (1 Cor. 10. 17), and of the mystery of indescribable union: 'no longer living to ourselves' (2 Cor. 5. 15) in order to live for those who love: 'indeed I live, yet not I, but Christ lives in me' (Gal. 2. 20). 'For God who commanded the light to shine out of the darkness, hath shined in our hearts' (2 Cor. 4. 6). A mutual indwelling love that is inconceivable to us for what it promised to us, beginning with the perception of the 'unveiled vision of the Lord's glory (as love)' and advancing to being a 'more and more glorious reflection through being changed into the same image of glory through the power of the Spirit of the Lord' (2 Cor. 4. 18).

IX

Love as Form

IF love can only be measured by love—if it cannot be measured by works which are at most its echo, or by faith, understood as the possibility of 'accepting something as true' and schizophrenically severed from love; or by suffering which may be involuntary, or sacrifice which may be self-righteous, or by any subjective experience (mysticism) which may be granted to someone who does not love—then it inevitably appears formless, outside our precise human world and indeed as a threat to the human order. That apparent formlessness, however, must be faced; for love is a perfect agreement with God's will and decrees, whether already known or still hidden from us; it means consent in advance to everything, whatever it may be: the Cross, abandonment, oblivion, uselessness, insignificance. It is the Son's consent to the Father, the mother's consent to the angel's message because he bears the word of God; the Church's consent and that of her members to their sovereign Lord: 'If I will . . . what is that to thee' (John 21. 22, 23). It is 'the mind of the Church', of the Church subjectively placed before Christ, and so objectively, as the norm for the mind of her members.

But the love of God comes and implants itself into this threefold *fiat*, this perfectly open and boundless consent, as 'the seed of God' (1 John 3. 9) and thus determines, shapes and informs the *fiat*: it is the Father's 'pleasure', 'plan', 'intention', 'decision', 'pre-determination' (Eph. 1. 1-11); within it the Son's mission is formed, and within this the Church's mission and within this again, the Christian's mission; while it is for the sake of the whole plan, that we have the whole structure of creation, with its innumerable individual forms in time and space. For the creation, the forms of nature, have developed and opened themselves in spirit and in love to the unending fruitfulness of grace, receiving their final form from above so that everything natural is reformed, recast and re-orientated.[1] The archetype of this whole development is found in the way Christ's human nature stands out—ecstatically—in relation to his divine person, from which he draws his human existence; the mission he receives from the Father forms not only his office and destiny as Redeemer, but the essential traits of his individual nature. He assumed a human existence in order to offer it entirely to God for the sake of man and the world, in order to unite God and man by dissolving, 'emptying' himself, so that through the resurrection he might receive the nature he had sacrificed (and the world) back from the Father, transfigured and eternal, to place both eternally in the hands of the Father.

This is the form of love and the form into which the Christian is baptized: he is baptized 'into union with Christ's death' and 'is buried with him, and lies dead, in order that, as Christ was raised from the dead through

[1] 'But I fall into dissolution amid the changing times . . . until I may be run into thee, purified and molten by the fire of thy love. And after that will I stand, and grow hard in thee, in my mould' (St Augustine, *Conf.* XI. c. 29-30, trans. W. Watts, 1631; Loeb ed., repr. 1960).

the glory of the Father, so we too might walk in newness of life' (Rom. 6. 3-4). This form can only be the eternal life of Christ which we can only enter through a perfect *fiat*. It is present sacramentally and objectively in baptism; and the Church, repeating the *fiat*, does so representatively for all who are baptized. Every Christian must ratify that consent fully throughout his life in all that he is and does, and must try, however ineffectively, to approximate to it existentially. Faith is that wholehearted ratification, and it has the form of true faith only when it accepts *a priori* as true all that God says and does, even though this should contradict his priggish, self-confident reason. Our hesitant attempts to answer are the attempts of our love to realize a fundamental self-surrender to God. To be free from the compulsion of sin is to be free for the service of God (Rom. 6. 12-14), in which man stands naked as in death, waiting to receive the new form given to him as his baptismal robe. 'For as many of you as have been baptized in Christ have put on Christ' (Gal. 3. 27); 'the new man, created accordingly to the measure of God' (Eph. 4, 24). We thereby put on the form of Christ's life: 'Put on therefore, mercy from the depths of your hearts, kindness, humility, meekness, patience; forbearing with one another and forgiving one another; if any man have a quarrel against any, as the Lord has forgiven you, do you also. And above all these things put on charity, which binds everything together in perfect harmony' (Col. 3. 12-14).

This final 'perfecting' is twofold: it opens man to the infinite and leads him towards a fulfilling unity. It is essentially form-giving, the *ultima forma* that confers meaning on the whole process of integration. But, as the last quotation in particular shows, this love is not just any love, but Christ's, the love of the new and eternal covenant; love in the form of 'heartfelt mercy', 'kind receptive openness', 'readiness to serve', 'meekness that does not defend itself', 'longsuffering patience', overcoming and enduring one's unendurable fellow men, forgiveness because God has forgiven—in short, the 'virtue' which is derived from the 'perfecting bond'.

The end and aim of the education of the Old Testament, which brings man into a frame of mind pleasing to God, is this love. In the course of educating him, it leads him through the realm of the natural virtues towards the divine form; but this movement is such that at the time one is only aware of the dynamic force which inspires it —i.e., one knows (through one's faith in the leadership of God) that the whole movement must be transcended, even though the final form remains invisible.

This educative process is apparent first in the sphere of politics where we see Israel, in the name of the power of Jahweh, making war against her neighbours and ruthlessly exterminating them; we see it again in the sphere of social ethics, where the rights of the poor and oppressed, clear from the first, are ever more inexorably defined by the prophets; we see it finally in the realm of individual ethics where the individual is taught to give up his desire to see and possess immediately, through adopting a higher point of view where the mills of God's justice grind slowly.

All this is true only as part of the dynamic movement towards Christ's form of love; thus while the Church encourages any post-Christian political social or ethical ideas which could lead men towards it, she herself clings obstinately to the final goal of perfection, which is to 'know nothing but Christ, and him crucified' (1 Cor. 2. 2). On the pretext of sanctifying political power the Church can never return to the Old Testament situation, and make use of the power achieved in the Old Testament to spread the love revealed in the New. That is the policy of the 'integralists' who interpret '*in hoc signo vinces*' as 'you will gain a worldly victory in the name of the sign of worldly failure'. The Church cannot even make an absolute of a programme of social justice—which would certainly be much more in conformity with the spirit of the New Testament—nor can she identify herself with such a programme in the hope of giving it a Christian colouring—as the Christian socialists do. Even the Church's proclamation of the principles of social justice, and any efforts she may make to realize them, must be steeped in the love of the New Testament, following the example of the apostles (2 Cor. 8-9; 1 John 3. 17; James 2. 1-5, etc.) and as Christ himself, the poorest of the poor, showed by setting himself (which is to say the outpouring of his love) above a reasoned and rational concern for the poor and the proletariat (John 12. 8), only on that condition can love for one's neighbour preserve its absolute character—be directed towards the Son of Man. St Paul was never tired of emphasizing that even the highest values of individual ethics were undermined without the love of God: love alone can fulfil the law, being its epitome (Rom. 13. 10; Gal. 5. 14). Without love, the law is no more than a negative barrier against sin (1 Thess. 1. 8f.); not even the faith that justified Abraham, not even the giving of all one's goods to the poor, which is Jesus' counsel of perfection, is 'anything' without love

(1 Cor. 13, 1-3), not to mention 'religious awareness'. It alone can help us to transcend ourselves and fulfil ourselves, and it alone is 'the more excellent way' (1 Cor. 12. 31) that forms both faith and hope (*ibid* 7). Everything in Scripture that is not love is a figure of love (Pascal).

The same is fundamentally true of the relationship between natural virtue and Christian love—whether the relationship is taken in a more negative sense, as by St Augustine in the *Civitas Dei* (where love is the only necessary form), or whether it is given a more positive sense (as the fulfilment of preceding forms). From this it becomes clear that all religions and philosophies tend, in their thought, towards ultimate human forms, and since they are rooted in man's natural relation to his creator, they may display traits similar to the final Christian form, reflecting it in various degrees of clarity; but an even greater dissimilarity cuts right across that similarity and is shown to us in the acts of the living God, his death on the Cross and resurrection.

Certainly, one must not overlook the virtues which can be derived from natural religion and *pietas* towards God: those virtues so highly esteemed in the Asiatic and Hellenic religions, for example: the restraining and thwarting of the passions, meekness, long-suffering patience, pure sympathy, a certain humility that avoids drawing attention to individual laws and interests, and a wisdom that gropes towards an understanding of absolute law and a sense of security even when exposed to the blows of fate. It is this sphere of high endeavour, with its teaching of 'the cardinal virtues': a bold, discriminating prudence, a fortitude confident in victory, a temperate, orderly sense of measure, a justice striving towards reason and providence, that lends order to the social structure, the family and individual life. Christianity leaves them of course unquestioned, and the Christian is simply called upon to fulfil them beyond measure. But this must be done in such a way that all four dimensions of virtue, and all the more exalted paths to God, are seen to culminate in a standard of judgment which of themselves these virtues could never achieve or grasp, and which therefore appears pure 'foolishness'; the profound sense of this standard must at first seem senseless, in order that its higher sense may be perceived, not through philosophy, but only in faith.

It is wisdom that sends a man into a Buddhist monastery in order to practise and acquire virtue through the sacrifice of his worldly goods. The Christian chooses a way that is outwardly analagous, but he does not ask to 'perfect himself', or 'to satisfy himself'—he is in love with the love that appeared to him in Christ. And it is only within that love that he can believe that his self-sacrifice, when joined to the sacrifice of the Cross, makes sense, because it is included in Christ's love. 'Turning the other cheek' is not primarily an ethical injunction—to teach us greater self-control or give an enlightened example of restraint—it is a counsel of love, which 'desires to experience the humiliation of Christ rather than gain respect or honour, which wishes to be looked upon as a fool and a clown for the sake of Christ who was so looked upon' (Ignatius of Loyola).

Natural virtue is always defined by what is sensible and reasonable, and since the person acting is part of the world order (*ordo universi*), by what is most sensible and reasonable for him. Within this order, love is based solely on the natural co-ordination of all the elements of life—being, working, feeling, suffering together; it depends upon the establishment of an equilibrium between the standpoint of the individual and that of his neighbour, of the individual and society, of the individual and the whole. But an absolute law of (Trinitarian) love has only to flash like a lightning stroke from the 'whole' as from the living God, and all these ingenious attempts at equilibrium are upset, because they are deprived of their claim to centrality and are called upon to reorientate themselves towards something outside themselves, something in fact which will from then on be the sole centre. It is the presence of that claim in the post-Christian world that makes any return to the harmony of the ancient world—where the world and the beyond corresponded naturally and easily—quite impossible. 'Whoever is not for me is against me' (Matt. 12. 30).

However it is equally mistaken to expect the form of New Testament love to provide an alternative—some new universal harmony. As we have been at pains to show, the principle cannot be derived from man as an organizing controlling centre: God remains the centre and man is related to something outside himself, to the absolute. Man only 'has' this love in so far as it 'possesses' him, that is to say he does not have it as a possession over which he has control, or which he can point to as one of his powers. Certainly it is not just external to him, but only because *it* seizes hold of him in the innermost depths of his person—*interius intimo meo*. It 'organizes' him, not he it; and it makes him—who always struggles against it—into an organ for the performance of its work.

And as he gets to know it, he will be careful not to say that he has it. At most he will venture to repeat the words of St John, in company with the Church the bride of Christ: 'we know that we have passed from death to life because we love the brethren' (1 John 3. 14). Christians who are sent into the world are sent on their way with authority and powers to confirm their message; but these powers do not draw attention to the messengers, they point to the Lord they are proclaiming. This is true even of faith, hope and love, in so far as they are intended to draw attention to God's form in the world. 'For we preach not ourselves, but Christ Jesus; and ourselves (we consider to be) your servants for Jesus' sake.' That is why this principle cannot embrace the work of the labouring world as a firm, easily graspable form, but only as the 'fragrance of Christ' blowing through the world, felt here and there but always escaping our grasp even when it announces something of the unendingness of love: 'to the one we are a fragrance from death to death; and to the other a fragrance from life to life' (2 Cor. 2. 15-16). A savour, a fragrance, but one which demands a decision, and lays bare the source of all future decisions. That is the one form of world culture possible since Christ.

The form of Christian love in the sign of Christ is indivisible; it can never be subjected to a sort of division of labour, some Christians specializing in the transcendent aspect (which is then called 'eschatological' or contemplative), others specializing in the immanent aspect (the active life, turned towards the world). Any hint of that dichotomy tears the image of Christ in two and makes it unrecognizable and incomprehensible in both aspects. It is 'agape' as a whole that shapes a whole life; whether under the laws of marriage or under the laws of a Christian refusal to marry, the second being the response to a more explicit call of Christ to a more explicit discipleship, and so to a more expressive imitation. In marriage the form of agape is superimposed on the sexual eros (and given the family, on private property and the free and responsible use of it). In life according to the evangelical counsels, which was Christ's form of life, the individual's existence is directly formed by agape in its pure form, the love between Christ and the Church, the bridegroom and the bride, united beneath the Cross, a union characterized by the poverty and obedience of the Cross.

There are not really three counsels, but one—to *one* form of life: nor are there really three vows, but only one—to vow oneself to the crucified form of love, as to the one and only form of life. At baptism all Christians are 'planted' into this form of life (Rom. 6. 3f); but the form of Christ in the form 'counselled'—*forma servi* (Phil. 2. 7; cf: Matt. 20, 27-28)—becomes a fruitful, formative *forma gregis* (an example to the flock) (1 Peter 5. 3), a *forma omnibus credentibus* (an example to all that believe) (1 Thess. 1. 7), and comes to represent the form of Christ for the Church and the world; and this 'serving' love 'ministers' to both forms, being itself the yeast that vanishes. For the formative power of Christ lies in the formlessness of the seed which dies and dissolves in the humus to rise again, not in its own form, as seed, but as an ear of corn (John 12. 24; 1 Cor. 15. 36, 42-44). This rhythm, the descent into the 'humus' with its humility and self-sacrifice, is characteristic of Christianity as a whole, and of its fruitfulness—but it is a rhythm which can be scanned variously, by the married or by the unmarried, the active or contemplative. It fulfils the messianic longing of the Old Testament to conquer the whole world, and still more man's instinct, planted in him by God, for the 'culture' of the world. But as far as the culture of the world is concerned, the seed Christianity has to offer only remains fruitful and can only germinate provided it is not identified with and encapsuled within some particular and illusory form, parallel to worldly and profane forms which, whenever they capture and monopolize it, condemn it to sterility. It must, like its founder, surrender itself completely, and sacrifice its particular form—without the least dread (*Angst*) in face of the dread of being let go and letting go of oneself. For if the world is to believe it can only believe in love.

X

Love as the Light of the World

CHRISTIAN love is not the world's last word about itself—it is God's final word about himself, and so about the world. In the Cross we see, above all, something foreign to the world, something which cuts clean across the worldly understanding: a Word which the world does not wish to hear at any price. For the world wants to live and rise again without dying; but Christ's love wishes to die, in order that, through death, it may rise again beyond death in God's form. This 'resurrection in death' is not a conception which can be annexed, added to, or put to use, by a world that dreads and flees death. But the world that wants to live before dying, can find no hope within itself (even in hopeless intellectual constructions), it can never eternalize the temporal.[1] God's word in Christ offers the world in its 'will to live' its one and only hope—in an utterly unforeseeable form, beyond the scope of the mind's constructions. In the eyes of the world, of course, it is a 'desperate' solution because it proposes death; but at the same time it reveals the hope-

[1] The immortality of the soul: But then what of man, who is body and soul? Or one of the various forms of the doctrine (Plotinian, Stoic, evolutionary) according to which the individual is absorbed into the whole—but then what about the person, the uniqueness of love? The transmigration of souls in one or other of its forms: this raises both questions at once.

lessness of the 'will to live', which cannot prevail against death. However, God's offer only appears desperate to a despairing 'will to live'. In itself God's offer is pure love, stronger in death than death itself—a love that 'overcomes' what the world struggles against in vain.

If the world allows these two despairs to neutralize one another, it discovers that the Word of God does not remain external to it but on the contrary brings it inward fulfilment, i.e., leads it whither willy-nilly it must go. 'Truly I tell you, when you were young you fastened your own belt and walked about here and there (*peripatum*) wherever you would; but when you become old you will stretch out your hands and a quite different one will gird you and lead you where you would not want to go' (John 21. 18). What is meant in this passage, by the different one? Is it immanent death—or the Cross? Or are we to understand that behind death—as the condition of its possibility—there is always the Cross? Does it mean that modern philosophy (Heidegger, Sartre, etc.), for ever coming up against death as the limit, must in the last resort be resolved upon death, and that it is in fact willy-nilly choosing the Cross? It cannot mean that the Cross is one of the categories of our world, a category which it is no doubt difficult to discover, but that once discovered provides the key to all forms of worldly being; or that the Cross is a sort of dialectical law of 'eternal dying and becoming' ('*ewigen Stirb und Werde*'), what Hegel called a 'speculative Good Friday', which empowers reason to take over and administer the word of God and incorporate death as a factor of life—so that reason appears as a sort of dialectical movement, for ever crucifying itself, and like the phoenix, recalling itself to life.

For if the Cross is turned into a law which reason can grasp and administer, even an elastic sort of law governing the rhythm of life, then it is once again a *law*—in the Pauline sense—and absolute love is displaced and set aside by knowledge: this means to say that God's sovereign freedom (which could be quite other than what it is) is judged before the court of human reason—and condemned as that which it really is.

The impossibility of following this line of argument does not however point to the other view, according to which 'knowledge' is handed over to the world by Christianity to become the province of philosophy and science, while man's encounter with the Word of God belongs exclusively in the province of faith—which is personal and cannot be justified in the sight of knowledge. For not only is there a genuine knowledge appertaining to faith (the gnosis so constantly stressed in the Gospels); it is also possible to reflect upon worldly being in the light of the knowledge of faith—to reflect upon the 'image and similitude' of created being, compare it with the divine archetype, and from this discover the water-mark of God's love in individual natures and in nature as a whole. But this sign, impressed upon nature, first comes to light when the sign of absolute love has appeared: then the being of the world can be interpreted in the light of the Cross; the inchoate forms and ways of love, which otherwise threaten to lead nowhere, can be elucidated in their proper, transcendental setting. But whenever the relationship between nature and grace is severed (as happens in the theory mentioned earlier, where 'faith' and 'knowledge' are constructed as opposites), then the whole of worldly being falls under the dominion of 'knowledge', and the springs and forces of love immanent in the world are overpowered and finally suffocated by science, technology and cybernetics. The result is a world without women, without children, without reverence for love in poverty and humiliation—a world in which power and the profit-margin are the sole criteria, where the disinterested, the useless, the purposeless is despised, persecuted and in the end exterminated—a world in which art itself is forced to wear the mask and features of technique.

If, however, we look at creation through the eyes of love, then we shall understand it—in spite of all the evidence that seems to point to a world devoid of love. We shall understand the creation not only in its essence, which up to a point it seems possible to explain through the internal relationships of nature, but we shall also understand the Why and Wherefore of creation, its very existence, for which no philosophy can ever find an adequate cause. For why, indeed, existence rather than nothing? And the question stands whether we affirm the existence of an absolute or not. If there is no absolute being, what can be the reason or meaning of these finite, transitory things in the midst of nothing: things which can never, on any theory or evolutionary principle, yield an absolute? But if there is an absolute, and if it is sufficient unto itself, why something else should exist is almost more incomprehensible. Only a philosophy of freedom and love can ever justify our existence—though not unless it at the same time interprets the essence of finite being in terms of love. Everything, in fact, must be interpreted in terms of love, and not in the final analysis, in terms of consciousness, or spirit, or power or pleasure and desire, or utility—all of which must only be regarded as ways leading towards, as the presuppositions for, the one fulfilling act that appears in overwhelming form in the sign of God. Beyond all this, the constitution of being (*Sein*) itself begins to reveal itself, at least in so far as it is nought but a 'yielding up of self'[2] into the finite and concrete, where finite being can only receive and grasp itself as it really is, as 'that which does not withhold itself'; by it finite being is initiated and introduced into the form of eternally-giving love. A growing self-consciousness, self-possession and grasp of being is only possible when our isolation and egoism begin to be broken down, when we enter the realm of communication, of exchange and of sympathy for mankind and the universe. The values of this world are only set in a true light when seen in relation to God's sign, because then the limits of love, the obstacles to it, are overcome, and the mystery of self-sacrificing love is safeguarded against the inroads of a knowledge that recognizes no limits.[3]

And above all man only becomes man when addressed in this context: singled out as a creature, as the person addressed, he comes fully to himself in his response. He is

[2] Cf. Ferdinand Ulrich, *Homo Abyssus* (1961); Gustav Siewerth, *Das Sein als Gleichnis Gottes* (1968); and *Das Schicksal der Metaphysik von Thomas zu Heidegger* (1959).

[3] The core of the great myths and mythical religions is preserved for us by the protective gaze of love: whether on being and beings, or in contemplation of genuine love between husband and wife and their love for their children, or in true friendship and patriotism, exposed though they are to destruction through hatred, betrayal or death, and to mysterious transformations, that submit to no recognizable law. Even in our demythologized world, the images are preserved for us, and it is from this source, the love of things, that new and credible images can at any moment emerge. Calderon showed how significant mythical images could be within the greater Christian image.

the language God uses to speak to him; how could he possibly not understand himself better in it than in any other language? Steeped in the light of God, he enters into his own clarity—but without endangering his own nature (by some form of spiritualism) or his creatureliness (through pride). Man is only made whole by God's healing.[4] In the light of the sign of God who annihilated himself to become man and to die forsaken, it becomes possible to perceive why God came forth from himself and became the creator of the world; expressing his absolute being and revealing as unfathomable love his perfect freedom, which is not an absolute beyond being, but the height, the depths, the length and the breadth of being itself.

That is precisely why the eternal priority of the divine word conceals itself in a weakness that accords priority to the one loved. God's love for his children awakens love in them, so that his love itself can become child, be born of its mother and awakened to incarnate love. The word of God calls forth man's answer by becoming an answering love which leaves the initiative to the world. The circle is complete and eternal: conceived and realized by God who is always above the world, and for that very reason remains at its centre. The heart is the centre of things, that is why special honour is given to the heart of Jesus, and to his head only when 'all blood and wounds', when it appears as the revelation of heart.

The long controversy as to whether eternal blessedness consists in contemplation or in love ends quite simply:

[4] See 'God Speaks as man' in *Verbum Caro* (1960, 73-99), *Die Vollendbarkeit des Menschen* and *Die Vollenbarkeit der Geschichte*—both published by Benziger (1963). [English trans., Herder and Herder, U.S.A., *Word and Redemption*—Tr.]

it can only consist in a loving contemplation; for what else is there to contemplate in God but love, and how else contemplate except by loving him?[5]

[5] This St Thomas knew full well, basing as he did the beatific vision on *connaturalitas*, which according to him depends rather on the *donum sapientiae* (which presupposes love) than on the *donum scientiae* (Cf. Raymond Martin, *Revue Thomiste*, Oct. 1909: 'Le principe formel de la contemplation surnaturelle'.)

Conclusion

LOGOS, as reason which understands, can only organize (*legein*) individual things, factual truths and 'dogmas' into an intelligible whole, by a process of selection, and by grouping them round a chosen point of reference. Where the revelation of God in Christ is concerned, the point of reference must be the same in both fundamental and dogmatic theology.

It is not to be found in cosmology (or in a religious ontology); for while philosophy and theology were in the past inextricably interrelated, the Reformation and modern times were perfectly justified in distinguishing clearly between them, although it was wrong to separate reason and faith in such a way that they ceased altogether to be related.

It cannot be found in anthropology, because man cannot be the measure of God, nor man's answer the measure of the word addressed to him.

It can only be found in revelation itself, that comes from God and provides the centre round which everything can be grouped. The ordinary run of Catholic theology places this centre on too low a plane for it to be possible to group the multiplicity of dogmas proposed to our belief effectively and convincingly round the unity of the Church's magisterium, which presents and justifies itself as founded by Christ, who for his part justifies himself as sent by the Father. The formal authority of the Church, and that of Christ, is ultimately credible only as the manifestation of the glory of God's love—this is real credibility.

The centre-point is equally put on too low a level in the alternative doctrine taught by orthodox Protestantism. In the place of the magisterium, it selects as the centre the demand for obedience from the self-authenticating, self-interpreting, word of Scripture: the Word in its twofold and existential form in the Old and New Covenants, as judgment and grace, law and gospel. This may be the formal structure of Scripture, but even as a whole it is only a witness to the concrete, incarnate God, who interprets himself as the absolute Love of God.

Liberal Protestant theology has perceived this clearly, for it presents Jesus of Nazareth, transcending the Old Testament knowledge of the two voices of God, the voice of his anger and the voice of his love, and revealing the Father's eternal love. But it goes on to make the revelation of the Cross and the Resurrection innocuous by transforming it into a banal 'teaching' or parable—instead of accepting the form itself realistically as the dramatic appearance of God's trinitarian love and as the Trinity's loving struggle for mankind. It was not a harmless 'teaching' that raised the already stinking body of the sinner from the grave that had been sealed for three days, and revived the flagging courage of the disciples, transforming them into witnesses to the Resurrection throughout the world.

The centre of reference put forward in these pages lies beyond the centres proposed by the theologies just mentioned. It is reached by gathering the *contents* of the kerygma into a single unity—neither gropingly nor vaguely, but in such a way that it has only one meaning. As can easily be seen, this centre-point embraces the other three and therefore shows itself—in this and no other way—to be the centre standing above any doctrine concerning man and the world. For, the formal authority of the Church's magisterium and of Scripture are neither of them impugned or weakened in any way by the glory of God's revealed love; on the contrary, it is the glory that finally confirms them and in theory and in practice establishes the obedience due to them on a firmer foundation. Only in the light of this twofold loving obedience to Church and to Scripture does the 'doctrine' of a loving God appear relevantly and convincingly as the mystery of love perpetuated in the here and now. What is more, no philosophical image of God is called in question; on the contrary, all our fragmentary knowledge is supplemented and completed when it is incorporated in the mystery of love. Moreover, the formal breadth of a philosophical view helps to prevent the theologian, the exegete and the ordinary believer from concentrating his attention so exclusively on the historical aspect of Christ's revelation that he ignores or forgets the action of the Holy Spirit. Finally, revelation does not disavow or denigrate our human, natural and supernatural aspirations, or disallow the fulfilment of our deepest desires, our *cor inquietum,* though it affirms that man's heart only understands itself when it has once realized that the divine love suffering for him on the Cross is turned towards him.

It is not because the spirit of man is sensual that love seems to come from 'outside', but because love can only exist between persons—a fact philosophy is inclined to forget. For us, God is the 'totally other' and appears to us in 'another': in 'the sacrament of our brother'. And it is only *as* the 'totally other' (than the world)—that he is at the same time, the 'not-other' (Nicholas of Cusa: *De non-aliud*), who in his otherness transcends the differences of this world—where 'this' is not 'that'. It is only because he is transcendent and above the world that he is in it. But the fact that he transcends us does not deprive him of the right, the power and the Word with which to reveal himself to us as eternal love, and to give himself to us and make himself understandable in his very incomprehensibility. *Consideratio rationabiliter comprehendit incomprehensible esse.*[1]

Theology seems, for the most part, to be turning in directions very different from the one suggested here. It is making great efforts to reduce the distance between Christianity and the world, and to enter into fruitful exchange with it. Centuries of wasted opportunity are being made good; and fundamental Christian truths are being formulated, which once expressed appear so right and obvious, that it is difficult to conceive how they can have been overlooked or forgotten for so long. Bridges which should never have been severed are being re-built, and still others built, that have been needed for a long time by contemporary intellectual and moral life. Consequences that should have been drawn long ago are being drawn from premisses which have always been there: for example, that if all men are called to supernatural salvation, grace must be active in them in some sense or other; that a dialogue between Christian and non-

[1] Anselm, *Monologion*, 64 (Schmidt, I, 75, 11-12).

Christian is possible and necessary within that grace; that not only the historical world, but the whole biological genesis of the Cosmos belongs in God's world plan and must be created and ordered towards the *anakephalaiôsis* of all things in Christ, towards the entire Kingdom of God.

Truths such as these appear overwhelmingly great to the Christians of today—and so they are. But that they should appear *new* is, for anyone who knows the Fathers, for example, somewhat surprising; for at bottom they are not new; not at least for those who have meditated on the great figures of Christian spirituality—Irenaeus, Origen, Erigena, Nicholas of Cusa, etc.—and have not allowed themselves to be misled by some narrow interpretation (e.g. Augustine's theology of hell, and Cyprian's interpretation of *extra ecclesia nulla salus*). It is in fact time, high time, that the Church's great spiritual tradition should at long last emerge and be recognized.

As a result however, and owing to our enthusiasm at having burst open so many doors, we are in some danger of allowing these delayed victories to obscure the heart of Christianity. The cosmological and anthropological deductions drawn by the Fathers of the Church and the great spiritual teachers are disposed round that centre as though in the form of a monstrance designed to hold up the eucharistic heart to our view. They are simply functions of that one centre, and lose their significance in providing a perspective of the world the moment the scandal of the Cross is blurred in the slightest degree. They were never an alibi for the thinkers of the past and never exonerated them even momentarily from the unceasing meditation on the mysteries of Christ, the Trinity and the hidden depths of the Church. They were emanations from the realm of genuine theology, penetrating into realms which in themselves belonged to *philosophy*.

As long as philosophy remained closely linked to theology, and the several sciences were still (in their undeveloped state) closely allied with philosophy, it was not difficult for a theologian to include in his purview, excursions into philosophy and the sciences. Nowadays this has become notably more difficult, and since a man can no longer be a specialist in all fields of study, the theologian who tries to play the specialist in biology, psychology, sociology and other anthropological sciences, may easily become a dilettante in his own field. Furthermore, his own 'speciality', theology, is a very curious one, for it not only presupposes that he devotes his whole intelligence to it, but his whole heart, behaviour, existence. This must provide a testimony, not for his humanitarian concern for his neighbour, but for his love for the mysteries of the Trinitarian God, and for the mystery of the Son of God crucified for him and for all men. He can never get beyond this 'material', and in any case he can never dominate it; he must, if he is to be a faithful servant in the administration of his office, use it so as to form or inform whatever formable material he may receive from the spheres of cosmology and anthropology. He can only do so, however (and this seems to be forgotten more and more), if he has received the purity of this form in adoring faith, and has allowed it to become incarnate in his own existence.

Where 'the discernment of Christianity' is concerned, it is probably best to start out from the assumption that we are (already) living in an atheistic, anthropocentric period and—as far as the Cosmos is concerned—in an evolutionary *milieu*. This world will not expect psychological or sociological or biological contributions from us Christians; it produces enough of its own. What, then, is the specifically Christian task? Not, surely, to busy oneself with peripheral questions, but with truths derived from the centre. And we cannot prepare ourselves too well, or fit ourselves too soon, to express these truths with the greatest degree of clarity at a level that is convincing.